THE
IMPRISONED
PRINCESS

THE SCANDALOUS LIFE OF
SOPHIA DOROTHEA OF CELLE

To granny Win, a truly classy lady!

THE
IMPRISONED
PRINCESS

THE SCANDALOUS LIFE OF
SOPHIA DOROTHEA OF CELLE

CATHERINE CURZON

PEN & SWORD
HISTORY

AN IMPRINT OF PEN & SWORD BOOKS LTD.
YORKSHIRE – PHILADELPHIA

First published in Great Britain in 2020 by
PEN AND SWORD HISTORY
An imprint of
Pen & Sword Books Ltd
Yorkshire – Philadelphia

Copyright © Catherine Curzon, 2020

Hardback ISBN: 978 1 47387 263 9
Paperback ISBN: 978 1 52676 310 5

Typeset in Times New Roman 11.5/14 by
Aura Technology and Software Services, India
Printed and bound in the UK by TJ International

Pen & Sword Books Limited incorporates the imprints of Atlas, Archaeology,
Aviation, Discovery, Family History, Fiction, History, Maritime, Military, Military
Classics, Politics, Select, Transport, True Crime, Air World, Frontline Publishing,
Leo Cooper, Remember When, Seaforth Publishing, The Praetorian Press,
Wharncliffe Local History, Wharncliffe Transport, Wharncliffe True Crime and
White Owl.

For a complete list of Pen & Sword titles please contact
PEN & SWORD BOOKS LIMITED
47 Church Street, Barnsley, South Yorkshire, S70 2AS, England
E-mail: enquiries@pen-and-sword.co.uk
Website: www.pen-and-sword.co.uk

Or
PEN AND SWORD BOOKS
1950 Lawrence Rd, Havertown, PA 19083, USA
E-mail: Uspen-and-sword@casematepublishers.com
Website: www.penandswordbooks.com

Contents

Illustrations

25. Sophia Dorothea's wing at Ahlden House.
26. The Coronation of George I.
27. Celle Castle.
28. Horace Walpole. Henry Hoppner Meyer, after Sir Thomas Lawrence. 1795.

Plates 1, 5, 9: Courtesy of The British Library. Public domain.

Plates 2, 4, 6, 7, 8, 10, 12, 13, 14, 18, 19, 22, 24, 25, 26, 27: Courtesy of Internet Archive Book Images. Public domain.

Plate 3: Courtesy of Universitäts-Bibliothek Heidelberg, under Creative Commons Attribution-ShareAlike 3.0 Unported licence CC BY-SA 3.0. https://creativecommons.org/licenses/by-sa/3.0/

Plate 11: Courtesy of The New York Public Library. Public domain.

Plates 15, 20, 21: Courtesy Wellcome Library, London, under Creative Commons Attribution only licence CC BY 4.0 http://creativecommons.org/licenses/by/4.0/

Plates 16, 28: Courtesy of The Yale Center for British Art. Public domain.

Plates 17, 23: Courtesy of Rijksmuseum, under Creative Commons Public Domain Dedication CC0 1.0 Universal licence. http://creativecommons.org/publicdomain/zero/1.0/deed.en

Acknowledgments

Telling the story of Sophia Dorothea has been a pleasure and a privilege. I'm indebted as always to the team at Pen & Sword, particularly Jon, who keeps the cake and gaming chat coming. Thanks also to my marvellous editor, Lucy, who continues to be as fierce and fabulous as tradition now dictates she should!

For everyone in every corner of the globe who has ever taken the time to read my royal tales, thank you for continuing to turn the pages. To Deb, Rob and Kathryn, may there be always pooches, pop and clappers galore - UTT! Adrian, open a bottle of something suitably decadent, I think Sophia Dorothea deserves it.

And top billing as always must be reserved for Pippa, Nelly, and the Rakish Colonial - the noblest of families.

Introduction

'The Unfortunate Sophia was confined in the castle of Alden, situated on the small river Aller, in the duchy of Zell. She terminated her miserable existence, after a long captivity of thirty-two years on the 13th of November 1726, in the sixty-first year of her age, only seven months before the death of George the First; and she was announced in the Gazette, under the title of the Electress Dowager of Hanover.

During her whole confinement, she behaved with no less mildness than dignity; and on receiving the sacrament once every week, never omitted on that awful occasion, making the most solemn asseverations, that she was not guilty of the crime laid to her charge.'[1]

The end is where we start from.

On 13 November 1726, the Duchess of Ahlden died. No more would she be glimpsed galloping around her estate on her steed, dressed in her finest gowns, diamonds glittering in her hair. No more would she be the spectre who peered over the shoulder of her husband, George I, nor the lost mother whose memory haunted her son, the future George II. No more would she look out on the world that had forgotten her and wonder, *what if?*

From a privileged childhood to a tumultuous marriage and a love affair that blazed so bright it threatened an electorate, Sophia Dorothea of Celle barely stopped to draw breath. Yet she is a footnote in the biography of her husband, a forgotten supporting player in the life of King George I. He locked her away hoping that the world would forget her and to some extent, he succeeded. Sophia Dorothea remains a shadowy figure in the history of the Georgian era. Today she rests peacefully in Celle's ducal burial vault and those who wrote the pages of scandal alongside her are all long dead, though not all have graves to call their own.

Introduction

This is the story of a girl who seemed to have it all and who, thanks to a dynastic arranged marriage that she had never wanted in the first place, found her life unravelling, the threads slipping through her fingers. It is the story of a woman who lost her children, her reputation and ultimately, her freedom. It is the story of a woman who might, under different circumstances, have become the first Hanoverian Queen of Great Britain. Instead she was a prisoner, her place taken by the king's mistress and her death barely noticed, let alone mourned, in the lost kingdom that she never saw.

But all of that is for the end.

What happened at the beginning?

Act One: Bride

'The daughter of a German potentate of little renown and less importance, a duke of the small territory of Zell, the lady brought to her husband a respectable fortune and an attractive person; her heart she did not bring him, for it was already given to another.'[1]

Don't expect a happy ending. This isn't that sort of story. It has all the ingredients of romantic fiction, from a handsome suitor to a damsel in distress and even a villainous, scheming lady pulling all the strings of disaster. Unlike fiction, however, our star-crossed lovers certainly don't get to ride off into a fairytale sunset.

In fact, the story doesn't even start with our star-crossed lovers, but long before they were born. The seeds of this particular disaster were sowed many years before there was a King George I, a Sophia Dorothea or even a dashing Count von Königsmarck. To understand where the trouble started, we must take ourselves back into the days of the Rhine Palatinate and Sophia, an unmarried lady in search of a husband.

A Game of Musical Fiancés

Once upon a time there were four brothers, each as ambitious as the last. They were the Dukes of Brunswick-Lüneburg: Christian Louis, George William, John Frederick and Ernest Augustus. In Heidelberg, meanwhile, was a very eligible young lady indeed. Her name was Sophia of the Palatinate. She was to catch the eye of not one, but two of those ducal siblings, and change the face of British history forever.

Sophia's life had not been a settled one. Her parents, Frederick V, Elector Palatine, and his wife, Elizabeth Stuart, were better known as the

1

Bohemian Winter King and Queen, so-called because the Holy Roman Emperor had warned ominously that Frederick would be 'gone with the winter snow'. Their short reign in Bohemia lasted little more than a year before a disastrous series of clashes with the mighty Holy Roman Empire sent the couple and their family into exile. So keen were they to flee that the deposed monarch even forgot to take his Order of the Garter, which he had been awarded by his father-in-law, King James I of England.

The relatively short life of Sophia's father was beset by drama and bad decisions and by the time he sought exile in The Hague Frederick was an exhausted if not broken man. His unfortunate decision to accept the Bohemian crown put him in direct opposition to the Holy Roman Emperor, who preceded him in Bohemia, and ended any influence he might have hoped to enjoy on the continent. When Sophia was born to the exiled couple who had made their new home in The Hague there was little rejoicing. As the couple's twelfth child, neither Elizabeth nor Frederick saw much novelty in her arrival. She was just one more mouth to feed. Indeed, just three months later any joy they might have felt at bringing yet another child into their already financially stretched family was doused by the death of the newborn Sophia's two-year-old sister, Charlotte of the Palatinate[2]. It was an inauspicious start to an eventful life.

Frederick died in exile when Sophia was just two and from that day until her marriage, her life was never particularly settled. Her mother, Elizabeth Stuart, far preferred the company of her pet monkeys and dogs to that of her numerous children. After Elizabeth's matchmaking efforts to betroth her daughter to the future King Charles II[3] came to nothing, the young lady was sent to reside at Heidelberg, court of her eldest brother, Charles Louis. It was here that she met two of those four ducal brothers from Brunswick-Lüneburg, George William and Ernest Augustus.

Ernest Augustus and Sophia took to each other straight away. They were of a similar age and discovered a shared love of the guitar, which they practised together for hours. If this was fiction we would be on track for a happy ending but in real life, the youngest of four brothers was far from the sort of husband that either Elizabeth Stuart or Charles Louis, who had become a second father to his younger sister, wanted. So the guitar sessions stayed at just that and after a little innocent strumming between friends, the couple went their separate ways.

But it seemed that neither Ernest Augustus nor Sophia were quite ready to break up the band just yet. They continued to correspond and Ernest Augustus sent his fellow musician some favourite pieces of guitar music which they discussed at length in their correspondence. With Sophia ripe for marriage, when her brother found out about these musical exchanges, he informed his sister that she must put away her paper and pen and stop writing to her friend. With Ernest Augustus having little chance of ever inheriting any real power as the youngest brother, Sophia's family was determined that she could do much better than him and an ongoing correspondence would do nothing to help her prospects with other potential suitors. Though she respectfully informed Charles Louis that, 'it would have been discourteous not to reply to thank him [Ernest Augustus] for the music he sent. Not to do so would have smacked of pride, which is itself a great sin'[4], the letter writing stopped.

And that, so everyone thought, was that.

Or not.

In fact, Ernest Augustus and Sophia were destined to collide again, though nobody could have guessed how.

George William, Ernest Augustus' older brother and best friend, *loved* to spend money. Both he and Ernest Augustus visited their beloved Italy as often as they could and there they indulged themselves in the proverbial wine and women, though they replaced song with gambling. If George William had ten coins, he could spend twenty. If he had a win at the card table, he loved nothing better than gambling with his profits and waiting to see where fate took him. In 1655, where it had taken him was into a black hole of debt.

George William's request for a greater allowance from the Brunswick-Lüneburg estates was not met with enthusiasm. The subjects of his duchy were already frustrated at their duke's frequent absences and his love of lavishing money on Italian ladies, card tables, and taverns, so this time they said *enough is enough*. There was to be no further payout for George William unless he at least made an effort to behave respectably. The first step on that road was to take a bride.

Though Sophia hadn't been without her suitors, none of them had come up with a marriage proposal and she was by now well into her twenties. This may make us modern sorts shrug our shoulders and ask: *So what*? but in dynastic terms, the child-bearing sun was swiftly setting on her and her prospects were growing dimmer with every passing month.

3

Not only that, but the fiercely intelligent Sophia was stifled by life in her brother's simmering court. Charles Louis and his wife, Charlotte, were at times literally at daggers drawn, with the electress engaged in a violent battle for her husband's affections with his mistress, Marie Luise von Degenfeld. It was a battle that she was destined to lose, but not before she nearly bit Luise's finger off and was caught heading to her rival's chambers with a sharpened dagger clutched in her hand. Naturally, Sophia responded by taking her adored brother's side in the ongoing dispute. Charlotte's response was to accuse the siblings of incest, a claim that she liked to repeat to whoever might care to listen.

Sophia had had it. A girl no longer, she was ready to make her own way in the world. She was ready for a husband and a home away from Heidelberg.

When George William approached Sophia and asked her for her hand, she didn't play hard to get. Though there was no question of being in love, marriage promised new surroundings, far from the intrigues of Heidelberg. As she recalled, 'Unlike the heroine of a novel, I did not hesitate to say yes.'[5]

As you may already have guessed, the wedding didn't happen. If it did, this would be an uneventful book.

With the matter of a fiancé resolved, George William set off for Italy and his diversions there. He had cannily decided not to inform the Brunswick-Lüneburg estates of the engagement straightway. Instead he preferred to negotiate on the question of money and decided only to reveal the existence of his fiancé when and if she became a useful bargaining chip. In fact, he was granted the money he wanted with no mention of the fiancé, and suddenly, he was in no rush to get to the altar. Instead, he happily fell back into his old riotous ways and whilst Sophia awaited the official word on her marriage plans, George William was painting the town a very vivid shade of red. He suddenly realised that he had made a terrible mistake, and whilst laid up with a rather eye-watering bout of venereal disease, he had a flash of inspiration.

George William didn't want to get married and he never *had*, it was all a means to a financial end. Now though, with nothing to think about other than the fun he might have with his Italian consorts once he was cured of his embarrassing ailment, he began to plot how he could escape his marital obligations and responsibilities all in one fell swoop.

The answer, George William decided, was obvious. His little brother and best friend, Ernest Augustus, was far more politically ambitious than he, not to mention just as single and just as eligible. In fact, Ernest Augustus and Sophia had got on so famously over their shared guitar duets that the answer had been staring him in the face all the time. Without seeking the lady's agreement, George William asked Ernest Augustus if he would like to marry Sophia instead. In return, he would agree to give his younger brother the territory of Lüneburg, which would satisfy the concerns of the subjects there who wanted a marriage and an heir. With that thorny issue resolved, George William would be able to hand over his responsibilities and get on with just enjoying life.

Ernest Augustus listened to the proposal with interest and was, it seemed, very keen on the idea. He requested one further concession though. As well as handing over the wealthy duchy of Lüneburg, he wanted George William to swear that he would not marry any other woman, no matter how long he lived. Ernest Augustus was a shrewd negotiator and he knew that should his brother later marry and have a legitimate son and heir, then that son might one day try to win back the territories his father had surrendered in his haste to escape the marital yolk. Rumour had it that George William's child-bearing days had been curtailed by his intimate infection anyway, but just in case there might be any doubt, Ernest Augustus wanted an official agreement detailing not only the territorial and bridal transfers but also his brother's promise that he wouldn't marry.

No problem, said George William, *consider it done*![6]

It was all presented to Sophia as a *fait accompli*, and she was pragmatic about the situation. She didn't love George William, after all, and wrote in her memoirs, 'the only love I felt was for a good establishment and [if] I could obtain this I would have no difficulty trading the older brother for the younger.'[7] Let nobody say she was sentimental!

Selling the new situation to the other ducal siblings was a bit more of a struggle than selling it to the bride-to-be. John Frederick, the third of the four brothers, was also unmarried and just like Ernest Augustus, he was a man who was looking to widen his influence. When he learned about the scheme cooked up by Ernest Augustus and George William, the second brother, he was fuming. He demanded answers from both of them, wondering why he had been overlooked in the negotiation for land and love - or something like it - but his protests were all to no avail. On 30 September 1658, Sophia of the Palatinate and Ernest Augustus, Duke of Brunswick-Lüneburg, were married.

For a little while at least, George William was a happy, happy man. He had passed his unwanted fiancé on to his brother, Ernest Augustus, and was merrily gadding about Italy with all manner of companions with nary a care in the world besides where the next party was being held. For George William, Duke of Brunswick-Lüneburg, life was positively merry. It didn't last.

Perhaps oddly, since he had been the one to reject *her*, the torch George William had never really carried for Sophia suddenly flared into life upon her marriage to Ernest Augustus. He became her shadow and every time she turned around, there he was. He was soon such a permanent fixture at Sophia's side that her husband became consumed with jealousy, convinced that his wife and brother were intriguing behind his back. So overwhelming were his suspicions that when he took his afternoon nap, Ernest Augustus made Sophia sit in the chair directly opposite his own. Then he placed his feet on the armrests of Sophia's chair, ensuring that she couldn't sneak away for a tryst whilst he was enjoying his siesta.

Sophia had little interest in her brother-in-law's dubious attractions but Ernest Augustus wouldn't accept that and George William couldn't bring himself to believe it either. He attempted to stumble into her room when she was dressing and when that failed, made sure that he was in Hanover every single time Ernest Augustus wasn't. At first, Sophia tried a subtle rejection, not catching her brother-in-law's eye and avoiding conversation with him, but he wouldn't be so easily dissuaded. In the end, it was time that wore George William down. Seeing that Sophia wasn't about to be won over by his questionable charms he went back to the other ladies of Europe, and was soon blazing a trail across the continent all over again.

As George William sowed his wild oats Ernest Augustus and Sophia were busy getting their house in order. The marriage had happened, now it was time for the heir and the spare, and they wasted no time in getting that particular ball rolling. Eventually the couple would have seven children who lived to adulthood[8]. The first son and heir, George Louis, was born on 28 May 1660, and for a time all seemed right with the world in Hanover.

So much for the king-to-be.

What about his ill-fated bride?

A Brother Betrayed

Sophia's path from Winter Princess to wife was, apart from the minor blip of changing bridegrooms, a fairly straightforward affair. With our little groom-to-be slumbering in his cradle though, the time has come to learn about the little bride-to-be. For *her* parents, marriage was anything *but* straightforward.

Sophia Dorothea's mother, Éléonore Desmier d'Olbreuse was born in 1639 at the grand-sounding Château d'Olbreuse in Deux-Sèvres. She was the daughter of a Huguenot family of minor nobility and she was a lady with ambition. Éléonore's status was way below that of Sophia, who was always rather smug in the knowledge that she was the daughter of albeit exiled royalty, not to mention the granddaughter of James I. She had bona fide royal blood flowing in her veins which Éléonore certainly didn't, but they did have a couple of things in common. Both had lost a parent in childhood - in Sophia's case her father, in Éléonore's, her mother - and both knew what it was to suffer exile. Sophia's *Winter Family* had been banished to The Hague after her late father's disastrously short-lived reign in Bohemia and whilst Éléonore might not be the daughter of a king, she too had been forced to leave her home behind.

Before all of this, however, Éléonore had a shot at the big time. Her widowed father, Alexandre, Marquis d'Olbreuse, decided to present his daughter at the glittering French court of Louis XIV. Wisely avoiding too much intrigue as she attempted to establish herself, Éléonore became a lady-in-waiting in the service of Marie Tour d'Auvergne, the ageing Duchess of Thouars[9]. She had a foot in the door at last and where better than the French court, where beauty and poise could take a young lady a very long way? These were two qualities that Éléonore had in spades, and the future looked very bright indeed.

So it might have been for Éléonore under different circumstances but no matter how charming the court found her, she was still a Huguenot. Just as it was for all of those who shared her faith, France was closing its doors to the house of Desmier d'Olbreuse and Éléonore and her father were forced into exile, their property and money seized.

Just like that, Éléonore's days at court were unceremoniously cut short. Though she had little to her name now, one thing Éléonore did still enjoy was her connection to the Duchess of Thouars, the

mother-in-law of Emilie, the Princess of Tarente. She accompanied the
duchess to the princess's court in Kassel and from there to Breda, in the
Netherlands. Breda played a particularly important place in the lives of
some seventeenth century royals as it was known as a city that welcomed
aristocratic exiles with open arms, ruled as it was by the Prince of
Orange, a supporter of the Stuart cause. Éléonore's father established
himself there and so did England's Charles II[10]. For the exiled Huguenot
marquis and his daughter, it was a natural place to settle.

It was at the court of the Princess of Tarente that that Éléonore
and George William met for the first time. Éléonore was predictably
beautiful, with a fashionably porcelain complexion topped by a brunette
mane, whilst her personality was charm personified. She was everything
George William now decided that he wanted, and he was determined to
win Éléonore's affections no matter what.

Faced with Éléonore's charms, George William's fancy for Sophia
evaporated like summer dew and the Hanover courtiers saw little of him
for a time. Instead he was to be found flitting about the distant court of
Breda, pursuing his new favourite. Seeking some scheme that he might
employ to snare her attention, George William asked Éléonore if she
would help him with his desire to improve his spoken French and she
readily consented. If French is truly the language of love then George
William had played a blinder and, during his lessons, his adoration for
Éléonore flourished. But if he was hoping to find it reciprocated with
abandon, he was to be disappointed.

Chased from the French court along with her fellow Huguenots,
Éléonore had nothing to her name but her honour and she wasn't about
to risk that to become another notch on George William's well-worn
bedpost. Éléonore certainly fell for George William, but she was a
little more reserved than the Italian ladies he had become so used to.
To surrender her reputation without the promise of anything from her
paramour was too risky to even consider but if she could secure an
understanding from George William, things might be very different.

George William, meanwhile, knew that he couldn't remain away
from home forever. The death of one brother had already occurred[11]
and his responsibilities were increasing, yet he didn't want to leave
without Éléonore and we might imagine that she was quite happy to
accompany him after all those innocent French lessons. Of course, the
one thing George William couldn't offer thanks to his agreement with

Ernest Augustus was marriage and if the lady wasn't willing to travel as his mistress, it was necessary to find a middle ground. That came courtesy of his sister-in-law, Sophia, who agreed to invite Éléonore to join her retinue at Iburg[12] as a lady-in-waiting. For Ernest Augustus, the arrangement could not be better. It meant he had his beloved brother nearby but without any need for jealousy, since George William would be too preoccupied with Éléonore to bother batting his eyelids at Sophia.

Éléonore duly arrived in Iburg and was warmly welcomed by Sophia. The two women got to know one another over salt biscuits and coffee but soon, reality began to bite. Hard. Sophia and Éléonore simply didn't get on, with the latter balking at just how seriously she was expected to take her role as lady-in-waiting. This wasn't the carefree and scandalous Princess of Tarente, but a duchess with Stuart blood in her veins, and Sophia expected to be treated accordingly. Éléonore had exchanged a court full of romance and intrigue for one where she dined with servants whilst her suitor sat at the top table, and she wasn't in the least bit impressed.

Éléonore wanted a husband but since George William couldn't make that wish come true, he offered her instead a generous package of incentives to become his mistress, including a payment of 2,000 crowns per year as long as he lived and 6,000 crowns per year following his death. Tired of the life of a lady-in-waiting, she finally agreed and off the couple went to bed, with Éléonore now recognised as an official mistress. Reputation mattered less to a woman with a fat pension waiting in the event of her older lover's death, after all.

With her status more or less official, Éléonore spent the night with George William. But when she emerged from her rooms the next day, the tears were flowing. Having slept on things, Éléonore informed Sophia, George William and Ernest Augustus that she wasn't happy. Though in her heart she *felt* married, she explained, to the rest of the world and in God's eyes, she wasn't. Perhaps, she ventured, were she to be known as *Lady Celle* that might go some way to fixing this little issue of honour. The trio said no, for the Dowager Duchess of Celle still lived and giving her title to George William's mistress would cause ructions to say the least. Satisfied that a title would be the end to it, for that earlier venereal disease had seen off George William's chances of fatherhood, they offered the alternative of *Lady Harburg*. Éléonore accepted.

Lady Harburg and George William were not to stay a two for long. Flying in the face of his supposed diagnosis of impotence, George William proved to be rather fertile after all and on 15 September 1666, Éléonore gave birth to a little girl. She was Sophia Dorothea of Celle.

Our leading lady.

Legitimising the Lady

Though technically Sophia Dorothea enjoyed no real status whatsoever, her doting parents treated her birth as though she was the heiress to the grandest throne in Europe. George William might once have signed away valuable territory to his brother to escape marriage to Sophia but now, under the influence of his bride, his property portfolio was growing and his coffers were filling up nicely. Because she wasn't a legitimate wife, Éléonore stood to inherit nothing from her husband except for the promised payment of 6,000 crowns per year, but George William's new interest in acquiring territory was building her a very comfortable nest egg indeed.

He acquired land and property with an admirable zeal and in Osnabrück, Ernest Augustus looked on with no small amount of envy. Shackled by his responsibilities as a leader and having been a little *too* free with his money in the past, now the purse strings were being tightened. In Celle, meanwhile, the spending went on seemingly without any cares whatsoever. George William, he thought, was getting the better deal. Ernest Augustus approached his brother and voiced his concerns until George William gave him a little something to keep him happy. That was a payment of 40,000 thalers, with the understanding that it was a tax as opposed to a bribe. There was further provision made for future such *taxes* against George William's territory, which he duly paid as required.

Tax, not bribe.

Of course it was.

And what of Sophia? The woman she had agreed to bring into her home as a lady-in-waiting now sat at the head of a glittering pseudo-court of her own, queening it in a manner that Sophia, so focussed on dignity and birthright, never could. She was the daughter of Elizabeth Stuart and here she was being outshone by an exile who had come from the court of the Princess of Tarente. Sophia was delighted by the odd bit of gossip and when she heard of claims that Éléonore had hoodwinked George William by pretending not to be a lowly attendant in France, but a personal and close friend to the Bourbon dynasty, she was not pleased. That fairly low-key lie did nothing to quell her growing dislike of Éléonore and she wrote to her niece, Liselotte[13], telling her, 'Never would any respectable girl have entered the house of the Princess de Tarente, for [...] she is not a person with whom any one can live and remain clean. [...] However, d'Olbreuse being a nobody, it does not matter much.'[14]

Éléonore wasn't going to stay a nobody for long.

She was a natural when it came to public relations and often paraded the streets of Celle with her little girl, showing her off to George William's subjects. As one they fell in love with Sophia Dorothea, little caring about her illegitimacy but instead getting swept up in the sort of royal baby fever that we still see to this day. As the years passed and Éléonore lost three further daughters to stillbirth, she began to reflect on what the future might hold for Sophia Dorothea, the child whose mother might be known as *Lady Harburg* but who enjoyed no title of her own. In the cut-throat world of dynastic marriages, Éléonore knew, that could prove to be a costly issue.

It was time to hustle.

When Sophia Dorothea was still in single digits, Johann Helwig Sinold, Baron Schütz, Chancellor of Celle, heard that Duke Anthony Ulrich of Wolfenbüttel was seeking a bride for his son, Augustus Frederick. Anthony Ulrich had unexpectedly come into power in 1666 when his father, Augustus the Younger, Duke of Brunswick-Lüneburg had died. Although Anthony Ulrich's elder brother, Rudolph Augustus, became the reigning duke, he had little interest in ruling and preferred to spend his days out hunting. Just as George William passed his own responsibilities on to Ernest Augustus, Rudolph Augustus passed his on to Anthony Ulrich, appointing him unofficial co-ruler.[15] The one thing Anthony Ulrich didn't have was a lot of was money, and in Celle, money was available in abundance.

In return for Sophia Dorothea's vast dowry of 100,000 thalers, Duke Anthony Ulrich offered respectability, prestige and rank, but there was one very big problem and that was the matter of the little girl's illegitimacy. Anthony Ulrich wasn't too much of a stickler for such things and, if the problem could be taken care of with a minimum of fuss, then he would be more than happy to give the proposed marriage his blessing. Yet George William still remembered the promise he had made his brother all those years earlier and was determined to keep it. He refused to go back on the agreement and marry Éléonore no matter what the duke wanted, and on that point he was immovable.

Until Éléonore worked her charms.

There was nothing Éléonore wanted more than to become the legal wife of George William, to set aside the bitter memory of exile and the courtesy title of *Lady Harburg* and become the Duchess of Celle once and for all. Sophia recognised her would-be sister-in-law's ambition better than anybody and had a feeling that Éléonore would get her way eventually, no matter what George William might think. When she heard that Leopold I, Holy Roman Emperor, had referred to Éléonore as a duchess, Sophia was incensed at such a liberty. The emperor and Éléonore were frustratingly chummy thanks to her efforts to ensure that George William lent the empire all the military assistance it might need in its conflicts. She knew how to make friends and she knew how to win influence.

Sophia, however, enjoyed little influence. Whilst Éléonore lived it up in Celle, she was busy being a good dynastic wife and providing her husband with plenty of spares to support the heir. That didn't stop her from taking up her pen and writing to Liselotte to reflect bitterly that, 'We shall soon have to say "Madame la Duchesse" to this little clot of dirt [Éléonore], for is there another name for that mean *intrigante* who comes from nowhere?'[16].

Clot of dirt or not, Éléonore was on the up.

George William simply couldn't refuse his beloved Éléonore anything, but he did try to find a solution that would suit all the parties concerned. He asked Ernest Augustus if he would be amenable to Leopold I, Holy Roman Emperor, legitimising the marriage on the understanding that there would be no negative impact whatsoever for Ernest Augustus. All he wanted, he explained, was for Sophia Dorothea to be able to use the arms of the house she were to marry into without having to add a *bend sinister*, a heraldic device that identified the holder as illegitimate. George William explained to his brother that Duke Anthony Ulrich wouldn't agree to any marriage unless the bride was legitimate and he promised he would ask for nothing else.

Employing the negotiating powers of George Christopher von Hammerstein[17], George William asked his envoy to assure Ernest Augustus that the marriage would be morganatic. This would mean that any children born into it would have no right to inherit title, rank of privilege from him and would not be able to mount a future claim to the territories he had surrendered all those years ago. Furthermore, just to set Sophia's mind at rest, he asked for nothing for Éléonore beyond the title of Countess of Wilhelmsburg. Ernest Augustus agreed to all of this. The one condition he refused was Duke Anthony Ulrich's request for everyone to pretend that the marriage had been legitimate from the very beginning. It was the only thing that Ernest Augustus balked at.

The two brothers signed an agreement[18] that at long last legitimised not only Sophia Dorothea, but Éléonore too. George William and Éléonore were finally officially married in 1676, but that wasn't an end to it. Éléonore had achieved most of what she had set her heart on, but there were still one or two things outstanding. Chief amongst them was her wish that Sophia Dorothea would be known as *princess*, even if any future children of the marriage were to be content with being known as the Counts and Countesses of Wilhelmsburg. This was agreed to on condition that any descendants would be exempt from inheriting any titles and privileges ahead of the sons of Ernest Augustus. In this way, they remained true to the earlier agreement, made when George William had passed his responsibilities and his fiancé on to his brother.

Now Duke Anthony Ulrich could at last plan the wedding he had pursued for so long and Éléonore, finally a bride and the mother of a recognised and fully legitimised princess, could sleep peacefully in her bed.

Or not.

It took a cannonball to end not only Éléonore's hopes of marrying her daughter off to a crown prince, but also the life of the crown prince himself. It happened at the Siege of Philippsburg on 9 August 1676, when Augustus Frederick, Anthony Ulrich's son and Sophia Dorothea's intended husband, died from the catastrophic wounds he sustained after a cannonball struck him in the head. All that hustling, all that scheming to get Sophia Dorothea legitimised had suddenly come to nothing. Anthony Ulrich assured Éléonore that all was not lost. He had another son who could step into the breach and marry her instead.

This time George William intervened. Though saddened at the news of the young man's death, when he learned that another candidate was already waiting to be pushed to the front of the queue once everyone had had a dutiful old mourn he was unsettled. Although Éléonore was keen to get the marriage on the road, George William asked for some time to think. He would make his decision when Sophia Dorothea turned 16, he decided, and this time, nothing Éléonore did would change his mind.

Little did anyone know it, but his decision was a fateful one.

It's time to meet the villainess.

The Wicked Woman

Every tale needs a villain. Sophia might not have liked Éléonore but a bit of snobbery hardly makes for a memorable baddy. Instead we need a schemer, a black-hearted, cold-eyed manipulator who will stop at nothing to get their way. Someone who, more than a century after her death, was still remembered as 'a bloated spider, out of sight of her victims, but ready to pounce upon them the moment they got entangled in the intricate web she had spun for their destruction.'[19]

Here's to unbiased nineteenth century biographers!

The lady in question, seemingly perched in her web awaiting a juicy fly, was Clara Elisabeth von Meysenburg. As the daughter of Count Georg Philip von Meysenburg, Clara had more in common with Éléonore than Sophia. Just like the Huguenot she too had been born to minor nobility and presented at the court of Louis XIV, hoping to make her fortune. Accompanied by her sister, Catherine Marie, Clara had instead found herself just one charming lady in a sea of them, and most of her peers were far wealthier and better connected than her. The wily von Meysenburg clan wisely regrouped. At Versailles they were small and inconsequential fish in a truly massive pond but if they were able to find a smaller court in which to flourish, they might become the barracudas they were at heart.

That smaller court was Osnabrück, where Ernest Augustus ruled as bishop alongside his wife, Sophia. For a woman like Clara it was the perfect canvas on which to realise her schemes and ambitions and she was determined that here, unlike at Versailles, she wouldn't be pushed into the background. The two sisters were attractive, accomplished and always followed the height of fashion. They favoured heavy make-up and flamboyant gowns and though both were consummate schemers, they were possessed of plenty of charm too. It was a weapon they employed to devastating effect at their Osnabrück debut in 1673 when they dressed as shepherdesses to perform a short entertainment of their own devising at a fete given in honour of Ernest Augustus.

Their pretty features shining in the moonlight, the siblings commanded the attention of their audience effortlessly. Here they sparkled in a way that they couldn't in France, where their ambition might be immense but their coffers and influence were limited. At Osnabrück, ambition and a pretty face could carry a couple of young ladies a very long way indeed.

Amongst the happy spectators were three men who would play an important role in the future of Clara and Catherine Marie. Of course, the gentleman at the centre of attention was Ernest Augustus and at his side were the governors of his son, George. They were Franz Ernst von Platen[20], the future prime minister of Hanover, and Johann von dem Busche, and they became husbands to the sisters. Yet both women had ambitions beyond simple marriage and between them, they managed to stitch up the entire court.

Clara's first move was into Sophia's household, where she became a lady-in-waiting. Made up to the nines and a glamorous picture of fashion, Sophia must have known that it was only a matter of time before Clara would catch her husband's eye. At eighteen years Sophia's junior, Clara knew it too. Soon the day came when Ernest Augustus succumbed to Clara's questionable charms and Sophia, his wife and mother to his many children, could do nothing but sit and watch it happen. Of course, she wouldn't dream of intervening because she never had, she simply saw this as her lot and lamented in her memoirs that a wife could hardly expect her husband to stay faithful once the bloom had gone from her rose. No, she decided, Ernest Augustus must have his fancies whether at home or in Italy and if Clara was the latest, then so be it.

Ernest Augustus and Clara became lovers whilst her sister, Catherine Marie, ably snared young George. Clara's husband was well aware of his wife's extra-curricular endeavours and he encouraged them, recognising that his own influence could only increase thanks to her bedroom antics. In fact, when both Sophia and Clara gave birth to sons in 1674, there were few at court who doubted that the brothers shared the same father in Ernest Augustus. Should there be any doubt remaining, *both* boys were christened Ernest Augustus too!

Clara's second child with Ernest Augustus was born the following year and was a girl named Sophia Charlotte, a moniker she shared with his legitimate daughter. Sophia Charlotte became one of George's closest and most trusted friends, eventually being awarded for her loyalty with the title of Countess of Darlington and the nickname, thanks to her corpulent frame, of the *Elephant*. That friendship with George later grew so intimate that it led to rumours - false, of course - of incest between the pair. The court just loved a juicy bit of gossip, the more sexually outrageous the better.

But rumours of incest are for the future. We now have our heroine and our villain.

All we need is a hero.

The Dashing Hero

Look up the word *dashing* in the dictionary and if the world was a fair place, there would be a picture of Count Philip Christoph von Königsmarck. He was the quintessential roguish hero, a soldier and adventurer with looks and charm to spare, 'an equal mixture of Mars and Adonis' according to his adoring sister. Even better, the Swede came backed with an excellent family pedigree as the son of Count Kurt Christophe von Königsmarck and his wife, Maria, herself the daughter of a count.

Born in 1665, the young Königsmarck had the blood of soldiers flowing in his veins. His father and grandfather had both distinguished themselves in battle over the years and when the elder count died on the battlefield in 1673, his name was synonymous with military prowess. Perhaps with this in mind, as a teenager, Königsmarck was sent to Celle to serve as a page whilst completing his education. Here he and Sophia Dorothea became friends and, in the centuries that have passed since they lived, that friendship has been reimagined as the birth of a love that would transcend all others. In this romantic retelling of the story they wandered the palace together and wrote 'forget me not' in the condensation on its windows, sealing their relationship for the day when they could meet again.

It's tempting to speculate on the ever-popular theme of doomed romance and as youngsters they were certainly friends though not, as some have since speculated, lovers either in the courtly or physical sense. That particular gossip was fuelled when the young couple shared a few dances at a ball but they were virtually children, little caring for love and marriage. It was nothing more than a dance. Ironically, years later it was another dance - this one far from innocent - that would set the wheels turning toward tragedy.

The von Königsmarck name didn't just mean military might, but power, glamour and a certain amount of dashing charm. By the time Philip was a young man, it was a name that conjured up scandal too. That came courtesy of his eldest brother, Karl Johan, the new head of the household. Of course, domesticity was the last thing on his mind.

Karl Johan had looks, charm, money and a lust for adventure. He sated it not only with the family business of warfare, but by travel too. The young count crossed Europe, gathering admirers as he went thanks to his flair for showmanship and what passed for entertainment at the time, such as taking on Spanish bulls for the sake of a kiss.

Trouble found Karl Johan during a trip to England in 1680, with his brother, Philip, at his side. With Philip and his tutor, Frederick Adolf Hansen, lodged at Faubert's academy, a finishing school for young men in the Haymarket, his sibling prepared to cut a dash through society. It was during this trip that the 21-year-old soldier took a fancy to Elizabeth, Lady Ogle, the teenage widow of Henry Cavendish, Earl of Ogle. The unconsummated marriage to Ogle had lasted just a year before the groom's death[21] and Karl Johan thought he might have found the perfect bride. Unfortunately for him, Elizabeth married again before Karl Johan had a chance to press his suit, this time to Thomas Thynne, a Member of Parliament. Elizabeth was the heiress to an enormous fortune and Thomas, who counted Longleat amongst his extensive property portfolio, was known by the nickname, *Tom of Ten Thousand*, thanks to his immense wealth. He was also two decades his wife's senior and though he didn't know it, his days were numbered.

On a February evening in 1682, as Thomas travelled in his coach along Pall Mall after visiting the Countess of Northumberland, 'Borosky, a Polander, shot him with a Blunderbuss, which mortify'd him after such a barbarous Manner that Mr *Hobbs*, an eminent Chyrugeon, found in his Body Four Bullets, which had torn his Guts, wounded his Liver, and Stomach, and Gall, broke one of his Ribs, and wounded the great Bone below, of which wounds he died.'[22]

The result was a scandal. The three men who had accosted Thomas Thynne, namely Colonel Christopher Vratz, Charles George Borosky and John Stern, were arrested and taken to Newgate. Although he wasn't present at the scene of the crime, Karl Johan von Königsmarck was also sought, suspected of being the man behind the plot - but he was nowhere to be found. The motive for murder was believed to be his passion for Elizabeth Thynne - or her money - and everyone in London society knew that the charming Swede had been pursuing the young lady despite the fact that she was already married.

It was suspected that Philip must have been privy to his brother's plans to commit murder and as the search for Karl Johan intensified, Philip was summoned by King Charles II to give an account of his sibling's movements. Though he claimed to have no knowledge of the murder or the whereabouts of Karl Johan, Philip did confirm that his brother had hoped to woo Lady Ogle before she married Thynne, but this was already public knowledge. It began to look as though the count might never be found and if he had already fled abroad, then he would surely have escaped justice. When all hope seemed lost, however, Karl Johan was spotted at Gravesend, arranging passage on a ship to Sweden. Perhaps the fact that he had waist-length hair made him particularly easy to identify!

Karl Johan was cool and collected. He was fleeing England, he explained, but only because he knew that he was the obvious suspect in the murder thanks to his long friendship with Vratz, and he wished to make his representations from a safe distance.

Sir John Reresby[23], who questioned Karl Johan after he was detained, was shocked to receive a visit from Monsieur Faubert, who owned the academy where Philip was lodged. Faubert explained that he was a rich man and asked Reresby whether there might be any way that the suspicions against Karl Johan could be made to evaporate, leaving no stain on his reputation. To his credit, Reresby, told him 'that if [Karl Johan] was innocent, the law would acquit him, though he were a foreigner, as well as if he were a native; but that he ought to be careful how he made any offers of that kind, it being rather the way to make a man of honour his enemy than to gain him as a friend.'[24]

With his friend's efforts to buy him out of trouble proving fruitless, Karl Johan joined those in the dock, charged with being an accessory to murder. The trial opened on 28 February. Despite the fact that prosecutors stressed the point that nobody stood to benefit from the death of Thomas Thynne more than Karl Johan, he was the only member of the group *not* to be found guilty. Though Vratz argued that his trial was not a fair one, he, Borosky and Stern were all sentenced to death. Karl Johan was acquitted but advised that he might like to think about leaving England at the earliest possible opportunity. Charles II, Reresby wrote, 'was not displeased to hear it had passed in this manner.'[25]

There were some who were of the opinion that Karl Johan owed his acquittal not to the evidence presented but to his money and status. John Evelyn, that consummate diarist of his times, had much to say on the matter of Vratz and Königsmarck, and there can be no doubt how *he* would have found, had he been part of the jury.

> '10th March. This day was executed Colonel Vratz, and some of his accomplices, for the execrable murder of Mr. Thynne, set on by the principal Konigsmarck [sic]. He went to execution like an undaunted hero, as one that had done a friendly office for that base coward, Count Konigsmarck, who had hopes to marry his widow, the rich Lady Ogle, and was acquitted by a corrupt jury, and so got away.'[26]

Evelyn was disgusted that Karl Johan had walked free. Reresby was a little more sparing in his comment on the count than Evelyn, but both agreed on one thing. Vratz went to his death with dignity. 'Seeing me in my coach as he passed by in the cart to execution,' Evelyn recalled, Vratz 'bowed to me with a steady look, as he did to those he knew amongst the spectators, before he was turned off; in fine, his whole carriage, from his first being apprehended till the last, relished more of gallantry than religion.'[27]

Evelyn took up the narrative to remark that Vratz told a mutual friend who accompanied him to the gallows, that he 'hoped and believed God would deal with him like a gentleman. Never man went, so unconcerned for his sad fate'[28]. The case seemed to hold a particular fascination for the diarist, who later paid a visit to see the corpse of the hanged man. He dutifully recorded it in his diaries, a ghoulish memory of the way things once were.[29]

Tom of Ten Thousand was laid to rest in a tomb decorated with scenes of his own murder. A lengthy and rather over the top inscription was intended to be carved on the tomb but the Dean of Westminster wisely vetoed it. As you can see from the Abbey's translation below, it would have needed a *lot* of space!

"Thomas Thynne, Esq. Near this marble, destroyed by an early death, lies Thomas Thynne Esq. of Longleat in Wiltshire, a man not unequal to his illustrious birth, upon whom his family bestowed great capabilities, and Nature an even greater spirit. With the greatest enthusiasm he nourished and championed religion, (which had been appropriated by the corrupting influences of the Romans), and the laws of his country, and the liberty of its citizens, and, on many occasions, those deeds undertaken by his compatriots on behalf of their faith, as well as the majesty of the Britannic Empire. He took in marriage Elizabeth, Countess of Ogle, of the most ancient and most illustrious Percy family, daughter of the Duke of Northumberland and sole heir. For this cause tears: that supreme envy is ever the companion of supreme felicity; German, Swede and Pole conspired together under one head, names unworthy of this marble: two of whom were members of the guard of Charles, Count of Konigsmarck; alas, what a wicked crime did they set in motion, these men picked out for violence and murder. One single nation was not sufficient to carry this out; three armed men, seated on horseback, under cover of darkness, rose up against a lone, unarmed man, who was sitting in his carriage, suspecting no evil; four lead balls exploded in his vitals, and this same number opened up a way out for his departing spirit. But punishment followed hard upon the crime, the assassins being apprehended not without divine assistance; found guilty of the palpable crime which the German had ordered, the Pole had executed, and at which the Swede had been summoned to assist, they all perished at the hands of the hangman. Moreover, the Count of Konigsmarck himself was sought, not only as an accessory, but also as the instigator; he was brought back from charge by the votes of the jurymen; two of the culprits, however, right up to their very deaths challenged the charge against him, while the third preferred to hold his peace."

And what of the newly-widowed Elizabeth?

She didn't let the grass grow under her feet. Less than six months after her second husband was assassinated, Elizabeth Thynne had very definitely moved on. Her next and last husband was no less a figure than the immensely wealthy and well-connected Charles Seymour, 6th Duke of Somerset. This was textbook social climbing of a rather bloody kind, and as Duchess of Somerset, Elizabeth became one of Queen Anne's closest and most trusted confidantes, eventually securing the role as her Mistress of the Robes. Though Elizabeth was mother to seven children by the duke, the marriage was ultimately miserable, regardless of how rich and pampered it might have been.[30]

Karl Johan was free to go his merry way, and he went back to his adventuring career. Though he may have escaped justice in the murder of *Tom of Ten Thousand*, his luck ran out in 1686 when he died whilst fighting in the Morean War. His brother, Philip, inherited his brother's title at his death.

Of course, none of the scandal could be attributed to Philip Christoph von Königsmarck but when his brother left England, so too did he. He had been expected to enroll at Oxford University but instead he found himself in France, where he continued his education.

Philip wasn't implicated in any murder or conspiracy but it certainly wasn't the sort of scandal that any young man would want going ahead of him as he started out in life. One or two of those rather fanciful commentators who romanticised Sophia Dorothea's story later tried to establish some sort of youthful love between her and Königsmarck, suggesting that the two had fallen for one another during his relatively brief stay in Celle but there was no such attachment. They might have been friends and even dance partners when necessary, but they weren't teenage sweethearts. When Sophia Dorothea eventually reacted with horror to her betrothal to George it wasn't because she would have preferred the young Swede, no matter how tragic and romantic that might have been.

Besides, after all her hustling and social climbing, the last thing Éléonore intended was to let her daughter, by now the proud bearer of the rank of *princess*, marry a count, no matter how adventurous and dashing he was. No, she had set her heart on the young crown prince of Wolfenbüttel and when that annoying cannonball ruined her plans, she had a feeling that all she had to do was wait, hoping that, on Sophia Dorothea's sixteenth birthday, George William would gladly accept Anthony Ulrich's offer of his next son.

Just in case that didn't pan out, Éléonore didn't burn all her bridges and she was sure to make it known that her daughter was a girl no longer, but 'exquisitely beautiful; her behaviour full of sweetness and modesty, her air noble and majestic'[31]. Celebrated as a 'brunette, with dark brown, almost black hair, large velvety eyes, regular features, brilliant complexion, and the veriest little red rosebud of a mouth,'[32] she was a catch indeed. Of course, 'her figure was perfectly proportioned: she had an exquisite neck and bust, and slender little hands and feet,'[33] and that wasn't all.

When it came to dynastic marriages looks were by no means everything and even Sophia Dorothea's thick mane of glossy brunette hair and milky skin wouldn't necessarily be enough to snare the best husband available. Yet when one added her enormous dowry and the fortune in land and money that she one day stood to inherit, she became the very definition of the *total package*. Sophia Dorothea, Éléonore decided, was not going to struggle as she had, chased into exile and scratching a living as a lady-in-waiting to aristocratic mistresses, though that fate was never one she realistically faced. With Éléonore in her corner, Sophia Dorothea was going to be the organ grinder, not the attendant monkey.

Although Éléonore fully expected that, on Sophia Dorothea's sixteenth birthday, Crown Prince Augustus William, Anthony Ulrich's oldest surviving son, would be at her door ready to pledge himself to her daughter, she was still keeping her options open. What she *didn't* know was that other interested parties were looking at Celle and they weren't parties that she would have been particularly happy to entertain.

The *clot of dirt*, it seemed, was about to be pushed aside by the sister-in-law who hated her, for ambition and cash had trumped snobbery once and for all.

An Ambitious Mistress

Éléonore was not the only ambitious person on the continent and as she had been plotting for rank and privilege, Ernest Augustus was one step ahead of her. His brother, John Frederick, died in 1679 and with another brother, Christian Louis, having predeceased him, that meant that what had once been split four ways was now down to two.

Ernest Augustus and George William were the only brothers left to steer the ship and since George William had long since signed over his more boring responsibilities to Ernest Augustus, that meant one man was now effectively in charge. Ernest Augustus inherited the title of *Prince of Calenberg* on the death of John Frederick, but he wanted more. For years he had thrown the support and might of his troops behind the Holy Roman Empire whenever it was required and now he wanted some payback for it. He fancied himself not just as a prince, but as an *elector*[34]. His mistress, Clara, had ambition enough for two and she knew just as well as Ernest Augustus did that the more land and clout he commanded, the more likely it was that he would succeed in securing the coveted status of electorate for his dominions. So far there had been no serious contenders for the hand of young George whilst in Celle, Sophia Dorothea, the girl with money at her fingertips and a father with territory to spare, likewise remained single.

For now.

If Sophia Dorothea and George could be brought together in wedlock, Ernest Augustus' power and George William's money could be united once and for all. Independently, the brothers had the ingredients to create the perfect recipe for an electorate. Together, they would be dynamite.

Clara, still the relatively lowly - in her eyes, at least - Baroness von Platen, knew that she had to handle this particular dynamite with kid gloves. Sophia loathed Éléonore and would no doubt balk at the thought of 'that bit of a bastard', as she called Sophia Dorothea, as a daughter-in-law. She had already fired her own matchmaking salvo though, dispatching her son George to England on a quest to win the hand of Princess Anne, daughter of James II[35]. The meeting had been a resounding failure and Anne was resolutely unimpressed with her would-be suitor, who had returned home with nothing to show for his troubles. Things in Celle were a little better and Éléonore had visions of her daughter snaring a crown prince from Brunswick-Wolfenbüttel as soon as Sophia Dorothea turned 16. The idea of her agreeing to a marriage between the two cousins was unlikely and she certainly had the ability to talk George William out of accepting it too.

The game was afoot, and Clara must move her pawns carefully if she was to achieve her dynastic aims.

Clara was not alone in her scheming though. She knew of a gentleman at the heart of the Celle court who could certainly be malleable when it came to achieving their shared aims. He was the prime minister, Andreas Gottlieb von Bernstorff, and he was more than happy to become her co-conspirator. Accepting as his payment an opulent gold snuffbox liberally decorated with glittering diamonds, Bernstorff agreed to subtly chat to George William. He would sing the praises of George, and he would do it whenever Éléonore was out of earshot. In Hanover Clara would be his equal, taking every opportunity to inform Ernest Augustus of the qualities and dowry of Sophia Dorothea, and always when Sophia was not around to hear. It would be pillow talk of a most dedicated, focused kind.

When Ernest Augustus first mentioned the idea of marrying the cousins to one another, Sophia dismissed it out of hand, but her influence over her own husband had never been particularly strong. Now this would prove to be her undoing, as Clara was suggesting a marriage for all the right reasons, and Ernest Augustus loved nothing more than power and privilege. By the time he spoke to Sophia about the prospective betrothal, Clara had convinced Ernest Augustus that it wasn't only desirable, but essential.

Happily for Clara, Sophia's own distaste at that 'little clot of dirt' who had married George William might be as strong as ever, but it wasn't as strong as her own ambition. Having grown up initially in the court-in-exile of her mother, Elizabeth Stuart, then at her brother's fiery household in Heidelberg, she knew too well of the privations of a cash-strapped court, and Hanover was increasingly becoming just that. She and Ernest Augustus didn't have much in common but one thing they did share was a passion for property and they had lavished a fortune on a brand new palace at Osnabrück, as well as extensive improvements to the gardens of Herrenhausen. That was before one considered the cost of the regular trips Ernest Augustus took to Italy, where he fell in love with the fabulous Venetian carnival. In fact, he loved it so much that he established Hanover's own carnival, in which glittering entertainments lit up the land for days.[36] All of this cost hard cash and as Celle grew richer, Hanover's finances were in decline. Sophia knew better than most that they needed an injection of serious capital.

As his wife counted the pennies, Ernest Augustus considered the matter of territory. As it stood, George William, 'a German potentate of little renown and less importance', as described by one 19th century commentator, had acquired quite a portfolio of land. Should Sophia Dorothea find an ambitious husband from another family, there was the lingering possibility that trouble could lie on the horizon. There would be nothing to stop that husband from mounting a take-over bid for the dominions that George William owned and if that happened, who knew what might follow? If the marriage kept things in the family, as it were, all of those possible crises could be averted in one fell swoop.

So it was that the household in Hanover reached its conclusion. George and Sophia Dorothea must marry and with the young lady's sixteenth birthday approaching, there was no time to lose.

Ernest Augustus had not forgotten how, years earlier, his brother had been Sophia's shadow. It had driven him to jealous distraction, after all, and had left Sophia despairing of her brother-in-law's odd behaviour. Now though, that devotion to Sophia was about to be turned against George William, for it was she who was dispatched to Celle to plead the case for the marriage. None knew if George William would agree to her request but the signs were good. Bernstorff felt confident of a happy outcome, having laboured admirably in return for his snuffbox, but the decision was ultimately George William's to make.

Above all else, it must not be left to Éléonore to have the final say in the matter of her daughter's marriage, for that would ruin all the carefully laid schemes. Whatever happened, she must be among the last to know.

Sweet Sixteen

On the eve of Sophia Dorothea's sixteenth birthday, Sophia left Hanover and travelled through the darkness towards Celle. Hers was a race against time and against Anthony Ulrich too, for he had waited years to claim the hand of the young princess for his son, patiently counting down the days until George William would make his decision.

The sun had barely risen over the horizon when Sophia reached her destination. Always a stickler for protocol, this time she let it be damned and eschewed official announcements and greetings, choosing instead to hurry through the castle towards her brother-in-law's bedchamber. The unsuspecting Éléonore still slept but George William was awake and Sophia waylaid him in the middle of dressing, so intent was she on her wake-up call.

Éléonore, snoozing in the adjoining room, was awakened by the sound of the new arrival and understandably asked Sophia what on earth had precipitated this unexpected and, one suspects, unwelcome visit. Sophia explained that she had simply wanted to be the very first person on the scene to wish Sophia Dorothea a happy birthday and unbelievably, Éléonore accepted the bizarre explanation. With her worries assuaged, she asked Sophia to excuse her as she dressed, no doubt wondering what had happened to cause the change in the demeanour of the woman who had been her most bitter rival.

As Éléonore dressed, Sophia urgently told George William of her ambitions for George and Sophia Dorothea. She knew full well that his wife couldn't speak Dutch and for that reason, it was the language in which Sophia made her representations, certain that Duke Anthony Ulrich must already be on the road to Celle, his bachelor son at his side. George William listened with interest, seeing in the scheme a way to renew his friendship with Ernest Augustus. Once so close, the relationship between the brothers had been weakened by the bitter battle between Sophia and Éléonore, not to mention Ernest Augustus' own annoyance at his sibling's constant slight amendments to the agreement they had once had. Let us not forget that the man who promised never to become a husband or a father was now indisputably both, after all. Yet if the young people were betrothed and their houses united by marriage, all of that might still be put right and the men might be confidantes once more.

Sophia was sure to mention the prospect of an electorate too and either by accident or design, George William seized hold of the wrong end of that particular stick. Though Ernest Augustus planned to see Hanover elevated to the status of electorate, George William didn't quite grasp this particular part of the scheme. In his head he began to picture the Electorate of Celle, with himself sitting at its head as the powerful elector.

It was a tempting proposition.

Occupied by thoughts of himself and his brother as best friends once more, the electoral cap of Celle perched atop his head, George William didn't stop to even consider his wife, let alone the patiently waiting Anthony Ulrich. Instead he said yes, he would pledge his daughter's hand to the eligible young man from Hanover. When Éléonore reappeared ready to greet her visitor and bring her daughter down to receive her birthday wishes, everything had changed for Sophia Dorothea. She was about to get the worst gift she had ever been given.

Éléonore was horrified, but George William wouldn't hear her complaints. The decision had been taken and all that was required of Éléonore was to break the news to Sophia Dorothea. The devastated mother fled to her daughter's rooms to bring her this most unwelcome of birthday gifts, leaving George William and Sophia to celebrate what they considered to be very happy news indeed.

In fact, Sophia had arrived not a moment too soon and as the in-laws settled to breakfast together, Anthony Ulrich arrived at the castle with his son, Augustus William. Fully expecting that today was the day the betrothal would become official, the party from Brunswick-Wolfenbüttel was taken through to meet George William and his unexpected companion. The pair was seated together as though they ruled Celle, with Éléonore and Sophia Dorothea nowhere to be seen, and they told the duke that he was too late, an engagement had already been arranged. Perhaps the men might like to stay for tea, Sophia suggested, and celebrate the birthday and betrothal all at once.

And the worst thing was Anthony Ulrich could do nothing at all to turn back the tide. He had no official agreement of anything from the Celle household, only the promise that they would consider a betrothal when Sophia Dorothea turned 16. Now that day had come, the betrothal had been considered and another had been found more attractive. Anthony Ulrich had been beaten by a far more audacious player, and the last thing on earth he wanted to do was stay for tea.

As the duke and his son left Celle and the scene of their bitter defeat, an even more bitter scene was taking place in the rooms of Sophia Dorothea.

Sophia Dorothea had been raised to hate all that the court in Hanover stood for. Éléonore had no love for Sophia and made sure to tell the girl that Celle was the place to be. Bright, wealthy and cheerful, she painted it as the polar opposite of the strict and austere world in Hanover, which was presided over by the sour and humourless Duchess Sophia. Of course, during those long years of competition with Sophia and Hanover, she had not expected that one day her own daughter would be destined for that very place. In encouraging Sophia Dorothea to count her many blessings, Éléonore had given her plenty of reasons *not* to want to visit Hanover. Now she wasn't only going to visit, she was going to make her home there.

Sophia Dorothea had no illusions about the character of her intended spouse either or if she did, they were swiftly to be shattered. George was not known as the life and soul of the party or as a man of great intellect. Though he would prove to be a keen soldier and a brave one too, when it came to matters domestic he wasn't what anyone would consider an ideal candidate as a husband. Put simply, he was boorish.

Disinterested in his education, sullen and difficult to know, let alone like, George had singularly failed to charm Princess Anne, thus putting an end to his mother's matchmaking with her ancestral English homeland. Of course, for a young man with matters military on his mind, the loss no doubt bothered Sophia more than it did him, since all George cared about besides the army was an outdoor life. Like his father, he loved to hunt and ride whilst his mother's passion for philosophy and education was utterly alien to him. We shouldn't doubt for so much as a second that Sophia Dorothea's own opinion of George was influenced by Éléonore's dislike of her in-laws. She had grown up learning not only of their austere court but of their unappealing son - that same unappealing son who was about to become her husband, for better or for worse.

Much worse, as it turned out.

All her life, Sophia Dorothea had been the apple of her mother and father's eyes. As their only child, she knew what it was to be doted on and whatever she wanted, she got. She was indulged to the point of distraction and had become high-spirited, willful and perhaps overly confident. At the age of 12, Sophia Dorothea's governess had secretly allowed her charge to exchange love notes with a young page. When the subterfuge was discovered both governess and page were sent packing, whilst Sophia Dorothea was essentially grounded and moved into her mother's apartments until she had learned the error of her ways. Such punishments were few and far between and it seems that the princess had danced through life, secure in the knowledge that her future would be a happy one.

Marriage was the pin that burst the balloon.

Upon learning what her fate was to be, Sophia Dorothea became heartbroken. Every dream she had enjoyed, every plan her mother had laid down for her advancement, were to be set aside in favour of this most unappealing of cousins. She might not have been in love with Anthony Ulrich's son but Éléonore had been sure to sing his praises at every opportunity. He was a tempting morsel and as far as Sophia Dorothea was concerned, he was her future.

And now he was leaving, whilst a messenger hastened to Hanover carrying word that the deal was done.

Duchess Sophia had not arrived in Celle empty-handed but had brought with her a valuable birthday gift for her niece. It was a painted miniature of George, held in an elaborately jewelled frame.

Once the party from Brunswick-Wolfenbüttel had departed, George William made his way to the rooms where his beloved and indulged daughter still sobbed in her mother's arms. He carried the miniature with him, determined to deliver Sophia's gift as well as to calm the distressed princess.

As far as gifts went, it wasn't her favourite.

As soon as she saw what he was carrying, Sophia Dorothea snatched the miniature from her father's hand. She flung it against the wall with all her might and bellowed, 'I will not marry the pig snout!'

She would, of course.

Even as Anthony Ulrich was heading in one direction, George was heading in the other. That sullen, snouty young man had been summoned to Celle to meet his new bride and celebrate the happy news of their betrothal. Though the groom seemed unable to muster much enthusiasm, Ernest Augustus could not have been happier. His wife had achieved her aim admirably and in that marriage, she had begun the reconciliation between the quietly estranged brothers. Now their houses and families would be joined once more and all could finally be well in Hanover.

Hopefully.

Daughters and Dowries

When George arrived in Celle he found that his welcome was anything but warm. Though George William was delighted to see his nephew, both Sophia Dorothea and Éléonore were nowhere to be seen. The young lady still refused to leave her chambers and her mother, furious at George William's lack of consultation on such an important matter, was locked away in there with her. George didn't care much anyway, since he hadn't wanted this marriage either. He was happy with his mistresses and the military though at least he could comfort himself with the thought that he would pocket a pretty penny in return.

'One hundred thousand thalers a year is a goodly sum to pocket,' wrote Sophia to her niece, Liselotte, though she reserved little sympathy for Sophia Dorothea, the 'pretty wife, who will find a match in my son George Louis, the most pigheaded, stubborn boy who ever lived, and who has round his brains such a thick crust that I defy any man or woman ever to discover what is in them. He does not care much for the match itself, but one hundred thousand thalers a year have tempted him as they would have tempted anyone else.'

Just like his father, George was always happy to follow the money. He knew all about balancing the books and he knew that he was likely to inherit all that his father now controlled, for Ernest Augustus had already begun to consider introducing primogeniture into the House of Hanover. Ultimately, this became the House's official path of succession in 1684, after much bad blood and wild water had passed under the bridge.

Although now only two brothers remained from those original four dukes, Ernest Augustus knew all too well of the kinds of problems that could arise when power was divided between siblings with ambitions and realms of their own, and he was determined that this wouldn't happen in his own family. As the father of six sons, he remembered vividly how disputes amongst his own siblings had led the family to the very brink of civil war when territory came up for grabs, and he had no desire to see history repeat itself among his own offspring. He knew too that the duchies of Brunswick-Lüneburg would be much more appealing as prospective electorates of the Holy Roman Empire if they were ruled over by a single man, rather than split between half a dozen. That chosen one, the eldest son, was George.

Sophia Dorothea, it seemed, was about to marry a man who stood on the edge of some very serious power. Thanks to the money, land and prestige that she would bring to the partnership, he was only going to get even more powerful and self-important. Yet Éléonore had no wish for her daughter to be unhappy, and she made a tactical decision not to do down George, but to talk him up. She urged the young woman to look to the future and count whatever blessings may be coming her way. When Ernest Augustus and George arrived at Celle to formalise matters, both mother and daughter excused themselves at first, leaving the men to celebrate alone.

Eventually Sophia Dorothea had to make an appearance. Sticking close to her mother, she was introduced to George and immediately affected a swoon. Whether it was a genuine emotional reaction or simply intended to make a point we can't guess but either way, it's probably not what a fiancé wants to see. George didn't really care though. This was his duty and he was determined to carry it out as quickly as possible, then get back to his real passions - the military and his mistress.

And Sophia Dorothea had made her point.

Though we can hardly expect Sophia Dorothea to have completely reversed her opinion of her husband-to-be, she did eventually come round or at the very least, she accepted her fate. Given what came later, it's very tempting to paint these early days in the most florid and purple manner, suggesting that the young lady was virtually dragged sobbing to the altar, her mother in floods of tears behind her, but that wasn't really the case. Though the manner of the betrothal was far from ideal, we can't forget Éléonore's steely eyed determination to achieve her own personal rise from lady-in-waiting to duchess. She didn't abandon these character traits when it came to the marriage of her daughter either, because above all else, Lady Harburg was always a realist. Though she comforted Sophia Dorothea when the news was first broken on her sixteenth birthday, it strains credibility to imagine that Éléonore would have allowed Sophia Dorothea to go on with her tantrums and temper indefinitely.

We cannot know exactly what transpired between Sophia Dorothea's birthday and the day of her wedding, but we can be sure that she didn't spend the time locked in her room sobbing into her pillow. As the child of a duke, she would always have known that her fate was to one day make a good marriage and once the dust of the shocking news had settled, mother and daughter would no doubt have come together to consider the many blessings that the match promised.

Unlike Éléonore, Sophia Dorothea would never have to battle for place and privilege, nor sit at the servants' table whilst her *betters* dined on fine foods. She was to marry a man who, if all went to plan, would inherit not only his father's duchies, but the longed-for electoral cap itself. Ernest Augustus had sacrificed his relationships with so many of his other sons to achieve that ambition and Sophia Dorothea, once the illegitimate daughter of an exile, might one day be his electress. Though a sense of romance might tempt us to pretend that it wasn't the case, Sophia Dorothea was marrying into potentially great things and Éléonore and George William would have known it just as well as she did.

Likewise, though some of Sophia Dorothea's biographers have painted a picture of Sophia as a wicked mother-in-law, devoted to making her daughter-in-law's life hell, at the beginning this certainly wasn't the case, and Ernest Augustus was charmed by virtually everything the young lady did. As the years passed both of these opinions changed but we shall come to that in good time and even then, we won't encounter the evil mother-in-law of those early biographies. In fact, Sophia did all she could to smooth Sophia Dorothea's arrival in Hanover and when Éléonore requested that Catherine Marie von dem Busche, the mistress of George and sister to the scheming Clara, be sent away, Sophia agreed. Though both women probably fully expected other mistresses to take her place, they could at the very least send Sophia Dorothea off on her marital way without any rivals living in the same palace.

This was not without repercussions. Clara wasn't used to dealing with counter schemes and she had long since come to take her sister's influence over George for granted. Now that influence was ending and all because of the arrival of the very woman *she* had encouraged Ernest Augustus to secure as a bride for his son. It was an early warning to Clara that she should take great care when dealing with Sophia Dorothea but more importantly, she knew that she must install another mistress of her choosing as soon as possible. In Hanover, the search for the candidate was on.

In Celle, however, there was no talk of mistresses, only brides. A month before her wedding Sophia Dorothea put pen to paper and wrote to Sophia to thank her for allowing her to marry George. It must have been a painful letter to write in some ways but Sophia Dorothea, a princess to her bones, knew all about making the right impression.

> 'Madam
>
> I have so much respect for my Lord Duke, your husband, and for my Lord my own father, that I shall always be content in whatever manner they agree to act in my behalf; and your Highness will do me the justice to believe so, and that no one can be more sensible than I am of the many proofs of your goodness.
>
> I will carefully endeavour, all my life long, to deserve the same, and to make it appear to your Highness, by my respect and humble service, that you could not choose as your daughter one who better than myself knows how to requite you. In which duty I shall feel great pleasure, and in showing you, by my submission, how much I am,
>
> Your Highness's very humble and obedient servant,
> SD'[37]

The letter's hardly dripping with delight and joy and if we read between the lines, might we detect a certain sullenness better suited to George himself? Perhaps, but perhaps that's simply seeing what we wish to, knowing what came after. Sophia Dorothea had been raised as a princess, prepared to marry a prince, and her behaviour - at this stage, at least - was impeccable. This letter stands as proof of that simple fact, if nothing else. It didn't matter if a noble girl got what she wanted, so long as she claimed to be profusely grateful for what she *did* have.

The wedding was announced amid great celebration and though Éléonore still mourned for what her daughter might have had if things had gone differently, she painted on a public smile as she thought of the prospects. Until now, there had still been no discussion as to whether the electorate would be Celle or Hanover but either way, joining the two duchies by marriage cemented the future of both. If there were reservations at home, the people of Celle were delighted for their princess and probably shared George William's own excitement for what this might mean for their land.

The marriage contracts were drawn up by none other than the scheming Bernstorff and Baron von Platen, Clara's husband. So happy to be reconciled with his brother in such a permanent manner, George William indulged Ernest Augustus' every wish and asked for few concessions on behalf of his daughter. One of the things she could expect to receive was the aforementioned 100,000 thalers, but this would be paid directly to her husband. Likewise George would take control of the lands that had been awarded to Sophia Dorothea in the agreement and she, to all intents and purposes, was entirely dependent on him for her living. Although she was to receive an annual payment of 4,000 thalers, it would be paid to George and it was up to him to decide how it should be spent.

Even if George died before Sophia Dorothea however, there would be no 100,000 thalers coming her way. The most she would receive would be 12,000 thalers which, though not a pittance, was a long way from what her husband stood to gain financially from the marriage. But there was much to be said for rank and prestige and Sophia Dorothea would be receiving both in spades.

On 22 November 1682, George and Sophia Dorothea were married at Celle. Though public festivities and celebrations had marked the betrothal, the ceremony itself was a rather more muted affair. The couple was wed in the castle's chapel before a congregation of parents and friends as a storm raged outside. In later years, the scene was reimagined as a Gothic tragedy of monumental proportions where 'everything was thought of but the bride, whose heart beat heavily and bitterly beneath the folds of a superb lace veil; nor could the most penetrating eye discern any visible emotion beneath the gossamer texture of her deadened white pall,'[38] but this is a rather fanciful Victorian scenario. Éléonore and Sophia Dorothea had resigned themselves to her fate and though images of Sophia Dorothea approaching 'the altar with the air of a martyr approaching an inevitable doom'[39] are deliciously lurid, it's important not to be carried away by such ideas. In fact, the wedding proceeded without any drama or interruption and everyone played their part to perfection. The following night, a ballet and opera was performed to celebrate the marriage before the couple watched a firework display in honour of their union.

It would prove to be a dark day indeed.

Coming Home

It was early December when Sophia Dorothea and George arrived in Hanover to begin the second stage of the marital celebrations. With her, Sophia Dorothea brought Eleonore von dem Knesebeck, her lady-in-waiting and confidante, and when their magnificent coach rolled into the city they were received by a populace in the mood to party. The decorated streets were thronged with Hanoverians who cheered a hearty welcome as the couple passed by, bound for the Old Palace in the centre of the city.

Catherine Marie von dem Busche, however, had not obeyed Sophia's command to leave before the happy couple entered the duchy. Instead the banished mistress remained just long enough to witness their arrival. Spotted by Sophia, she was given her marching orders again and this time she obeyed. The path was clear at last, and the newlyweds could finally concentrate on getting to know one another.

The festivities continued for days and everyone who met Sophia Dorothea fell for her. She was mistress of her own household for the first time and soon found that the laid-back court at Celle was a very different sort of place to the puffed up world of Hanover. One didn't get to become an elector without acting like one and Ernest Augustus and Sophia had created a world of protocol and pomp in which everyone was expected to know their place and behave appropriately. Appropriate behaviour, or the lack of it, would get Sophia Dorothea into all sorts of problems later.

Ernest Augustus and his brothers loved Italy and above all, they adored Venice. In his efforts to make Hanover a land befitting the status of electorate, Ernest Augustus took the example of the French and Venetian courts as the model for his own lands. The Leineschloss and the residence at Herrenhausen were both extensively re-modelled and the latter was, without a doubt, intended to conjure a dream of Venice in Hanover. Ernest Augustus' late brother, John Frederick, had employed an Italian architect, Giacomo Quirini, to rebuild Herrenhausen in an Italian style at an enormous cost and following his death, Duchess Sophia took one look at the unfinished project and saw only potential. For the remaining decades of her life Sophia doted on the garden and under her caring watch, it became one of the most magnificent sights in Europe. In their unstinting efforts to create the Venice of the North, Sophia and Ernest Augustus even had a canal dug at Herrenhausen around which they recreated the carnival that Ernest Augustus adored and gondolas piloted by specially employed Venetians were a common sight at court.

The grounds of Herrenhausen were everything to Sophia. They were her retreat in times of trouble and her joy in times of happiness. Fittingly, in 1714, the peaceful garden to which she had devoted her life was also the place in which she drew her dying breath.

But that wasn't to come for a long time!

The first indication that things might be going awry came when Sophia Dorothea showed signs that she was struggling with the strict system of etiquette that ruled in Hanover, which had seemingly modelled itself on the complex world of Versailles protocol. Though Sophia tried her best to steer her new daughter-in-law through this bewildering world, the young woman was as obstinate as her mother and just as Éléonore had once determined to become a duchess, so too did Sophia Dorothea swiftly determine that she would abandon Sophia's stultifying and beloved etiquette in favour of the more relaxed way of life she had known in Celle. Though her mother-in-law didn't quite balk at this, it was an early warning that she was far from at home in Hanover, and was also far from being the most accomplished princess in Europe.

Then she met Clara, the woman whose sister she had effectively displaced.

She couldn't have wished for a more dangerous foe.

Clara had revelled in occupying a place at court that was second only to Sophia but this new arrival took precedence over a woman who was ultimately no more than a long-term mistress, no matter how ambitious and scheming she might be. Having come from a court where husband and wife were as devoted to one another as one could hope in the world of seventeenth century noble marriages, Sophia Dorothea had had virtually no exposure to mistresses and zero experience of how a mistress might fit into a dynastic marriage. Besides, Clara had no claim over George, so Sophia Dorothea was determined to exert her place in the order of precedence.

Things might not have been perfect, but they were far from disastrous. Sophia Dorothea and George were on civil terms at the very least and on 30 October 1683, she did her duty and gave birth to the first heir while her husband was away on a military campaign. The little boy was christened George Augustus, though he became better known to history as King George II. He cemented Sophia Dorothea's place in the heart of her father-in-law, Ernest Augustus. Indeed, Sophia even cared for the newborn child when Sophia Dorothea and Ernest Augustus went to Italy to join George. It was Sophia Dorothea's first trip to a foreign country and when she arrived in the midst of carnival, she was determined to have the time of her life.

George had inherited his uncle and father's love of Italian vistas and, we might suspect, Italian ladies too. But it wasn't George who was about to attract some scandal, it was his wife.

Whilst enjoying the delights of carnival, Sophia Dorothea met Armand de Madaillan de Lesparre, Marquess de Lassay. A noted and eccentric *Don Juan of the Grand Siècle*, Lassay was famed for his amorous exploits[40] and he revelled in the company of the continent's most beautiful women. When he saw Sophia Dorothea, the crown princess herself, he was determined to seduce her. Though no proof existed to verify his claim, he was soon boasting that he had taken her to bed.

When news of Lassay's crowing reached Duchess Sophia in Hanover she was horrified, but Clara was the surprising voice of reason. She soothed Sophia's anxiety and told her that Lassay was known not for the truth of his statements, but their entertainment value. Nobody would believe it, she assured her lover's wife, and Sophia allowed herself to be soothed. In Italy, however, her son was far from happy at the rumours and for the first time, the cracks began to show. It's a good thing that Sophia wasn't alive to see the day when Lassay published the love letters he had supposedly sent to Sophia Dorothea though as a commentator wryly concluded, 'It has not yet occurred to the ever-busy autograph fabricators on the continent to forge the supposed replies of the princess.'[41]

For George though, the damage was already done. He hadn't wanted Sophia Dorothea to come to Italy in the first place, but instead had hoped to spend his time there entertaining himself just as his father and uncle had done for years. Sophia Dorothea's arrival effectively put the brakes on that plan but he knew as well as she did that the birth of the heir was not the end of the story. The *spare* was required to complete the set and George was keen to dispense with his obligations as quickly as possible, so he could get back to actually enjoying life. When Sophia Dorothea returned to Hanover she was pregnant again. It was her final pregnancy and, arguably, marked the end of the couple's intimacy.

The Road to an Electorate

The news of Sophia Dorothea's pregnancy was received in Hanover with great celebration by almost everyone, but for Clara it was one more sign that she needed to wrestle back some control from the crown princess. Ernest Augustus kept nothing from his mistress and we can be sure that if he knew of the cooling of his son's affections towards his wife, then so did Clara. No doubt she listened as any good lover should - nodding in all the right places and making reassuring replies whilst at the same time plotting to use the knowledge to her advantage. Her sister was gone and for now, George had no mistress. Clara, however, was determined to change all that.

Her first move was to go for the obvious candidate and quietly summon Catherine Marie back to Hanover. Yet George had been a younger man with comparatively little intimate experience when he first fell for Clara's sister and now, it seemed, her charms passed him by. He paid no attention to his former mistress whatsoever and Clara went back to the drawing board. Somewhere in Hanover, she was sure, was the lady who would appeal to George and in winning his heart or at least his loins, would become Clara's eyes and ears in the crown prince's inner circle.

This became more important than ever in 1684 when Ernest Augustus formally recognised primogeniture as the method of succession for his own titles and territories. It was a vital building block in the duke's attempts to raise Hanover to an electorate, for it meant that there would be no messy scramble for power between his sons if he was to die after becoming elector. His brother, George William, recognised exactly what was behind the change and knew now that Sophia had not been entirely honest when she made her unexpected dash to Celle on Sophia Dorothea's sixteenth birthday. Only now did he realise that Celle had never been the intended electorate that she had discussed with him. It had been Hanover from the start.

George William, the man who had given his word never to marry or have a child, had been outplayed by the woman he had once rejected. Game, set and match to Duchess Sophia.

At home, the move towards primogeniture had sent a shockwave through the ducal household. Although Ernest Augustus assured all his sons that they would receive generous payments even if they would not share in the rule of the familial territories, they were furious. The brothers saw only that their birthright had been snatched away and handed to George, the firstborn, and no amount of platitudes or cash would make up for it. Most outraged of all was Frederick Augustus, the second son, and he was sure to let his father know about his fury. He did his best to enlist his mother's support for his cause and things became so bitter at home that Ernest Augustus eventually threw his second son out, forcing him to forge a new life for himself.

'Poor Gus is thrust out, and his father will give him no more keep,' wrote his mother, who felt the departure of her son keenly, 'I laugh in the day, and cry all night about it; for I am a fool with my children.' That consummate schemer Clara von Platen, on the other hand, was a fool for no one.

Syphilis and Milk Baths

Clara wasn't getting any younger and after a lifetime of heavy make-up and rich living, she wasn't getting any prettier either. What she *did* have in spades was influence and though Ernest Augustus presided over Brunswick-Lüneburg, *she* presided over him. Thanks to her machinations, her husband was now titled Baron and would soon be elevated to Count. All who knew Clara knew full well that the richly favoured peer owed his high rank, not to mention his place in Hanover's inner circle, to his wife's endeavours.

Clara was still plotting in 1687 when Sophia Dorothea gave birth to a little girl who shared her name[42]. Though the safe delivery of the newborn was celebrated, there should be no doubt that there was disappointment that the new arrival was not a boy.

George was rarely what we might call happy but on the few occasions that he was, he was generally on a battlefield. This obviously carried inherent risks and though the next in line to the dukedom was little George Augustus, there was still no spare to support the heir. There was no question that a girl could inherit the duchy of Brunswick-Lüneburg so ideally, there would have been at the very least two sons, although half a dozen might have provided a bit more of a safety net in the event of disaster. For George though, there would be no safety net, as he and Sophia Dorothea would have no more children.

When Frederick William, Elector of Brandenburg, died in 1688, Ernest Augustus rubbed his hands in glee. Frederick William was a traditionalist, the sort of ruler who might choose to get in the way of the elevation of a duchy to an electorate. It seemed as though the fates were moving the pieces of this particular jigsaw just as Ernest Augustus wanted. The future looked rosy and if there was to be an electorate, then one day, George would inherit it. Clara saw it too, relishing the power and sway that she held over the older man. With the writing on the wall for his eldest son and her own sister long since banished from Hanover, how might she go about regaining her influence over George too?

How indeed?

In the centuries that have passed since this story took place, much has been made of the unabashed wickedness of Clara. She has been raised to the figure of a fairytale evil queen, a bitter creature scheming and plotting in the corner with no motive other than her hatred of the beautiful, innocent, doe-eyed princess who threatened her position at the top of the tree. All of this is, of course, retrospective, and the idea of mistress as broker of court gossip and scandal is by no means new. Much has also been made of Clara's brassy appearance, her fading looks and her waning influence but there's absolutely nothing to suggest that her sway over Ernest Augustus weakened for years and she remained his principal mistress until the day of his death. By that stage her role was one of companion rather than lover, but the point is important. For us to believe that Clara hated Sophia Dorothea because the young lady posed a threat to her position, we have to first establish that Sophia Dorothea *did* and to put it bluntly, she actually didn't.

Ernest Augustus certainly liked his daughter-in-law and enjoyed her company, but not in a way that might suggest he fancied her as a mistress in place of Clara. Likewise, whereas some histories of Hanover paint Duchess Sophia as a malicious figure lurking in the shadows, determined to undermine her daughter-in-law, what possible reason could she have had for doing that? She had contrived to bring about the marriage for the sake of her husband's ambitions, to raise his duchy into an electorate, and the last thing she would have wanted was for anything to upset that ambition. Sophia of Hanover had long since learned to tolerate her husband's mistresses, his trips to Italy, and his blatant flaunting of his relationship with Clara. She had set her sights on the dual role of mother and duchess, ensuring that the household worked like a well-oiled machine and involving herself as little as possible in court intrigues and politics. All she had wanted was for Sophia Dorothea to do the same.

So Clara might not have had any convincing reason to be jealous of Sophia Dorothea on a personal level, but she certainly knew better than anyone the importance of keeping her influence over the boss. She remembered all too well the humiliation of being run out of Paris by Louis XIV's favourites and of being an unimportant fish in a pond for which she was vastly undersized. Now she was the shark, and this was her ocean.

Though Clara was without a doubt a woman to be reckoned with, she became so infamous for her role in Sophia Dorothea's eventual fate that once upon a time it seemed as though there was a scramble to provide the most monstrous story about her imaginable, with those who made a saint out of Sophia Dorothea falling over themselves to make a wicked witch of Clara. My personal favourite contains milky shadows not only of Cleopatra but also the legend of Countess Elizabeth Báthory[43], and as so many things are with Clara, its veracity is doubtful but it's not *quite* entirely impossible to believe!

Clara's high-rolling lifestyle and love of cosmetics had supposedly left her fighting a war on two fronts. On one, years and years of wearing heavy make-up had resulted in skin that resembled the surface of a flaky moon. On the other, a long-term battle with the effects of syphilis was ravaging what had once been a handsome countenance, leaving her in the sticky situation of having to rely on more make-up to hide her disfigurement. She eventually hit on the idea of bathing in milk[44] in an effort to undo or at least slow down the damage. However, this did nothing to increase her popularity amongst a populace who couldn't always afford to drink milk, let alone to wash in it. Clara, however, had a solution that would benefit all parties. Once she had finished bathing her syphilitic body in the now far from fresh milk, she had it distributed to the poor along with a chunk of bread.

Generous to the last!

It is an unflattering portrait that has followed Clara around from the earliest days of Sophia Dorothea's most adoring biographers. She has become the evil queen from a fairytale, immortalised by William Makepeace Thackeray as Ernest Augustus' 'old, painted Jezebel of a mistress' and a 'hideous old court lady'. Whilst it's true that Clara was nearly two decades older than Sophia Dorothea, her crone-like qualities have been somewhat overstated in the interests of creating a suitably rotten villainess.

One of the most eye-opening and Gothic stories that attached itself to Clara over the years demonstrates perfectly how history has judged her. Clara had in her household a young lady named Ilse[45] who was elevated above the position of servant and served as something close to a companion to the countess. Ilse was young and beautiful and, we imagine, had little need for the heavy cosmetics with which Madame von Platen disguised the ravages of her hedonistic lifestyle.

Witty, smart and filled with the confidence of youth, Ilse soon caught the eye of Ernest Augustus during one of his many trips to Clara's residence at Monplaisir. That moment came on a summer afternoon when he discovered the young lady sitting in the shade of the trees and for a few minutes, he settled beside her and the couple enjoyed a conversation. Though Ilse was soon ready to excuse herself, Ernest Augustus bade her to remain and chat a while longer, little suspecting what the outcome would be.

When Clara saw the couple enjoying an apparently intimate exchange in the seclusion of the trees, she was apoplectic. Filled with fury, she swept out into the garden and told Ilse in no uncertain terms to go straight indoors. As soon as Ernest Augustus had left for home, Clara called for her servant and dismissed her from the household. If that wasn't enough, Clara didn't only sack Ilse, but had her imprisoned and held in the spinning house, a jail in which female prisoners were put to work. It is a quintessential bit of villainy: the older, jealous mistress condemning the younger, innocent girl to a miserable existence, and it fits perfectly with Clara's reputation.

With Ernest Augustus out of the way on duchy business, Clara appealed to her husband to authorise Ilse's incarceration and of course, he did so. Nobody argued with the word of such a senior official so Ilse was held for some time in miserable conditions without charge or trial, whilst her persecutor did her best to think of a suitable misdemeanour on which to have her tried. Ilse had broken no laws and eventually all that Clara could settle on was a wooly complaint that her servant had behaved without suitable moral fibre and gravity. It was hardly enough to have Ilse kept in prison but it was enough to have her banished from Hanover. A small victory, perhaps, but a victory nevertheless and more importantly, a clear indication of the power that the infamous Clara von Platen commanded.

Drummed out of town, the unfortunate Ilse wasn't about to be cowed. In fact, she was furious. She went straight to Ernest Augustus and demanded reparations and the restoration of her tattered reputation. If she had thought him the master of his mistress though, Ilse was to be sorely disappointed. Ernest Augustus did as little as he could to help her, short of doing nothing at all. Perhaps fearful of rocking the boat with Clara, he made a small payment to Ilse and advised her that she would be better off leaving Hanover rather than attempting to seek any further justice. In fact, he commented, she should probably be counting her blessings because things could have been much, much worse.

Unlike some of the people in this tale and certainly unlike many of the ladies who found themselves with neither home nor reputation, Ilse managed to forge a happy ending. No doubt mindful of the lack of love that existed between the ladies who presided over Ernest Augustus and the woman who was so beloved in Celle, she next requested an audience with Éléonore, Sophia Dorothea's mother. Upon hearing her tale of woe, Éléonore welcomed Ilse into her service as a lady-in-waiting. It was a poke in the eye for Clara, who never liked it when someone got the better of her.

That was certainly a black mark against Sophia Dorothea.

Her family was getting far too big for its boots.

The Count Comes to Hanover

Sophia Dorothea was now a mother of two and the neglected wife of one. George, to be blunt, couldn't be bothered. His mother did all she could to get along with Sophia Dorothea and, having lost her own daughter to marriage in 1684[46], she was glad to have the young lady so close at hand. Sophia always seemed to have a protégé of sorts, from Liselotte to her daughter, Sophia Charlotte, known as *Figuelotte*, and eventually her granddaughter-in-law, Caroline of Ansbach[47]. Had Sophia Dorothea been of the right temperament, it's reasonable to think that she might have filled the role of companion to Sophia admirably but, ultimately, she was cut from a different cloth. She had spirit to spare, which Sophia liked in her protégés, but she also liked an adherence to rank and protocol and that was where Sophia Dorothea would fall down.
Fatally.

Count Philip Christoph von Königsmarck arrived in Hanover in 1688, looking not for love but for fresh adventure. Ernest Augustus was impressed by the new arrival's military record and offered him the position of colonel in the Hanoverian army, which Königsmarck was delighted to accept. Whether he had any interest in rekindling his friendship with Sophia Dorothea we don't know for sure but he would certainly have known that she was now a princess in Hanover. However, it's more than fanciful to imagine that he deliberately came to Ernest Augustus' court hoping for romance, for it had been a long time since the two had met and when they had, they had been nothing more than teenage pals. Besides, Sophia Dorothea was a married lady and Königsmarck had plenty of female friends. One in particular, Charlotte Dorothea Rantzau of Holstein, had captured his heart and he hoped to marry her. Charlotte Dorothea was the daughter of a Danish count but the marriage wasn't to be and the young lady died when she was just 20, long before she and Königsmarck could become husband and wife.

Königsmarck and Sophia Dorothea came face to face again in 1688, when he attended a masked ball at Hanover. They were delighted to be able to catch up but that's where it ended. As far as they or anyone else was concerned, catching up was all it was.

Still, for a wealthy adventurer like Königsmarck, friends in the right places could work wonders. Perhaps his ambition at first was simply for a bit of networking but soon he and Sophia Dorothea were friends once more. By now shown virtually no attention whatsoever by her husband, it must have been bittersweet for Sophia Dorothea to be reminded of earlier, less complicated days. She confided in Königsmarck, who would have been in no doubt that the young wife was bitterly unhappy in her marriage, and he provided a sounding board alongside Eleonore von dem Knesebeck, her oldest and truest friend. One can only imagine what he must have thought when she told him how bad things were.

Königsmarck was everything that George wasn't. George didn't like to spend money too freely but Königsmarck did exactly that. He lived in a magnificent house, owned an enormous stable of fine horses and loved to spend lavishly. It all brought a bit of glamour to Hanover, which Ernest Augustus appreciated, even if George did not.

The new arrival knew how to win friends and influence people, and among those won over was a certain painted lady.

The Glorious Revolution

Thousands of miles away in England, the landscape of Duchess Sophia's ancestral home was changed forever by the Glorious Revolution, which would prove to have implications for the United Kingdom that echoed down through the centuries. It all began when James II, who had converted to Catholicism, and his second wife, Mary of Modena, welcomed the birth of their son, James Francis Edward Stuart, Prince of Wales. Better known to history now as *the Old Pretender*, James was baptised into the Catholic faith by his devout father.

Unfortunately, not everyone shared James' faith. At the thought of another Roman Catholic king waiting in the wings to succeed to the throne, an influential group of seven Protestant nobles stepped in and wrote to William, Prince of Orange, and husband of James II's daughter, Mary, and invited him to land in England and claim the throne for himself. The seven promised that they would throw their military, financial and political might behind any such move, thus ensuring William would be victorious.

Though the men were few in number their influence was immense and between them they covered not only the length and breadth of England, but both the Whig and Tory factions too[48]. Wielding considerable political power were Henry Compton and Thomas Osborne, 1st Earl of Danby. Compton promised the tacit backing of the Church of England whilst Danby, once a senior political figure during the reign of Charles II, could bring substantial support in the north of England and a wealth of political experience.

Charles Talbot, 12th Earl of Shrewsbury, was a high profile convert from Catholicism and William Cavendish, 4th Earl of Devonshire, commanded immense support in the Midlands. Richard Lumley, 2nd Viscount Lumley, brought with him not only influence in the army, but also in the north-east, whilst Edward Russell had considerable clout in the navy. Making up the seven was Henry Sydney, the man who wrote the letter. Sydney's brother, Algernon, had been commissioner at the trial of King Charles I, though he had opposed the execution of the monarch. Despite this, when Charles II was restored to the throne, Algernon was tried for treason and executed. He was remembered by his supporters and family as a martyr and for Henry, the chance to finally see the back of the Stuart line was a temptation that proved impossible to resist.

William arrived in England with an army, ready to claim the throne by force if necessary. James II, confident of victory, rejected an offer of military support from King Louis XIV and readied himself for battle. Yet he was to be surprised, because when the Orange party landed, they were joined not only by James' own daughter, Princess Anne, but by defecting Protestant soldiers too. James was outmatched and he knew it.

Luckily for the king, William of Orange wasn't in the mood for war and he turned a blind eye just long enough for James to flee to St Germain and the protection of the French court. He was succeeded by William and Mary and their joint reign ended the Catholic rule in England.

> 'Yesterday the Prince and Princess of Orange were proclaimed King and Queen of *England, France* and *Ireland*, and the Territories thereto belonging at the usual Places as *Whitehall, Temple-Bar*, and the *Royal Exchange;* the Ceremony as splendidly performed as ever there was before; there being all the Knights, Marshals men, the Heraulds [sic] at Arms attended by the Maces. At *Temple-Bar* the Lord Mayor, Sheriffs and Aldermen, with divers Persons of Quality on Horseback; also four regiments of the Trained Bands. But what was most observable, was the

innumerable Multitude of People, the Streets and Windows filled from top to bottom, Echoing forth their shouts, all crying, *God Save the King and Queen.*'[49]

With their position now consolidated, the new monarchs agreed to the Bill of Rights in 1689. This was an Act of Parliament that laid out and limited the powers of the joint sovereigns and established the powers of crown and Parliament and the right of free speech. It also formalised the fact that England would never again have a Roman Catholic ruler as 'it hath been found by experience that it is inconsistent with the safety and welfare of this Protestant kingdom to be governed by a papist prince.' This meant that the line of succession would change, shouldering aside more than fifty Catholic heirs in favour of the next Protestant branch on the tree. That branch happened to contain Duchess Sophia, the Protestant daughter of Elizabeth Stuart.

The Bill of Rights contained no mention of Sophia's name nor the family from Hanover either and, should a child be born to William and Mary or Mary's sister, Anne, the next in line to the throne, then Sophia's chances of inheriting the English crown would be pushed further back with each new arrival. Though William and Mary, who were first cousins, had been married since 1677, they had no children and Mary had suffered a miscarriage early in the marriage. Likewise Anne and her husband, Prince George of Denmark, had already lost six children[50] in infancy or to stillbirth and miscarriage. Yet Anne was still young and Sophia, herself a mother of seven who had experienced miscarriage, knew that the chances of Anne and George having more children were high.

And they did.

'On Saturday in the evening the young Prince, Son of their Royal Highnesses the Prince and Princess of *Denmark*, (whom His Majesty has been pleased to declare Duke of *Gloucester*), was Christened by the Lord Bishop of *London*, and named *William*, the King and the Earl of *Dorset* Lord-Chamberlain of His Majesty's Household, being Godfathers, and the Lady Marchioness of *Halifax* Godmother.'[51]

Should he live then the newborn Prince William, Duke of Gloucester, would step into the line of succession ahead of Sophia and her own family. The pragmatic duchess never expected to be queen anyway, for the chance of William and Mary *and* Anne and George remaining childless had been slim at best. She was still in the line of succession though, and that was all that mattered. Ernest Augustus, who envisioned little chance of ever seeing his spouse as Queen of England *did*, however, see a way that this unexpected development could be turned to his own advantage.

King James II, exiled in St Germain, was not necessarily willing to sit quietly on his hands and across Europe, sides were being taken. Holy Roman Emperor Leopold and Louis XIV stood on opposite sides of their own lines in the battle for continental supremacy and each knew that the considerable armies of Hanover and Celle might prove invaluable when it came to achieving victory.

Louis XIV had already sent his troops into the Palatinate, the lands once ruled by Duchess Sophia's ancestors and kin, and the invasion had been brutal. The country was ransacked and the people displaced but Ernest Augustus, despite his spousal interest in the wellbeing of the people of the Palatinate, didn't jump into the fray with Leopold to defend his wife's ancestral lands. In this early act of the Nine Years' War, he knew that family loyalty might not secure the best outcome, and Ernest Augustus was all about the endgame.

The French invasion sent shockwaves across Europe, as everyone wondered where Louis XIV's troops might tread next. Alliances were made that might once have been unimaginable and Emperor Leopold, a Catholic, formed an allegiance with the newly-enthroned William III of England, a Protestant. Leopold wanted the support of Ernest Augustus' armies but so did Louis XIV, whose own son was married to Sophia's beloved niece, Liselotte. Ernest Augustus knew how to play the game of diplomacy and he offered the emperor his allegiance on the condition that Hanover was at least considered as a possible candidate to become the ninth electorate of the Holy Roman Empire. Leopold hesitated but, perhaps mindful of Sophia's place in the line of English succession, William III took up the cudgel with the emperor on Ernest Augustus' behalf. He would do all he could on behalf of Hanover, he promised, if only the duke would swear his allegiance to the Grand Alliance[52].

To show how serious he was about his promise, in summer 1689 William dispatched Sir William Dutton Colt to take up his new role as the first ever English envoy to Celle, Hanover, and Wolfenbüttel.

Charged with winning the support of the rulers of those duchies for the Grand Alliance, Colt was unimpressed with what he found in Celle, but in Hanover, things were different. Colt wrote that the duchy 'has much more the appearance of a court, and the town being much larger and finer [than Celle], people laying out their money in building and furnishing their houses, besides abundance of strangers resorting constantly hither.'[53] Before a week had passed, Colt was writing again to exclaim that, 'Nothing can be happier than we are here, all the court and ministers showing us all imaginable kindness.'[54]

And it was all for a good reason, because the more glitter and influence Ernest Augustus could manufacture, the more likely that he would be able to press his advantage towards becoming the ninth electorate. It was just a matter of time now, he knew, and he was determined to make it in style.

Eventually, with the sound of Louis XIV's marching legions ringing in his ears, Leopold agreed. When the matter of conflict was settled, he would see what could be done about Hanover's ambitions to become an electorate. Ernest Augustus knew that there was no going back now that he stood on the threshold of seeing his most fanciful dreams come true.

It was time for a party, and to set the stage for scandal.

Act Two: Lover

'I adore you charming brunette, and I will die with these feelings, if you do not forget me, I swear to you that I will love you all my life.'[1]

Nobody knew how to play the courtly system as well as the Baron and Baroness von Platen and when they were elevated to the status of Count and Countess, their importance and influence was clearer than ever. Clara was the very model of subservient womanhood to her lover but to those beneath her, she was a figure to be reckoned with. She understood the intricate politics of the court better than perhaps any other woman at Hanover, and none knew with more certainty how to wield power.

By this time, Clara was the mother of two children of her own by her lover, Ernest Augustus. The first was a boy who shared his name and the second a girl, Sophia Charlotte[2]. In the years to come she would become one of her half-brother George's closest confidantes. Known as *the Elephant* thanks to her stout build, there were those at court who thought that she was George's mistress as well as his half-sibling, but there's nothing to suggest that these rumours were true.

With Sophia Charlotte being a decade Königsmarck's junior, Clara thought that he might be an ideal candidate to marry her daughter. Although ultimately nothing came of this plan, Königsmarck didn't entirely escape the clutches of Clara. With great interest she received reports that Sophia Dorothea had been walking in the gardens with her young son who, after a long day of play, was finally ready to rest. Sophia Dorothea scooped the little boy into her arms and carried him towards the castle. Unfortunately she had underestimated the weight of George Augustus and when Königsmarck saw her struggling to carry her young charge, he swept in and plucked the child from her arms, dashing to the last. This exchange struck Clara as a worryingly intimate one and she related it to Ernest Augustus, who dismissed the report as nothing but a gallant chap lending a helping hand.

Yet Clara had a streak of jealousy as long as the Leine, the river on which her lover's castle stood. Approaching middle-age and long since bored with the gout-ridden Ernest Augustus' less than enthusiastic bedroom antics, she saw in Königsmarck the sort of young man who could give a lady a very good time. Not only that, but to seduce him would be to get one over on Sophia Dorothea, as well as gain some power over the count too.

Power was on lots of minds in those days. William III, sitting comfortably on the throne of England, was acutely aware of the rattling of French sabres just over the water. Louis XIV had offered sanctuary to his dethroned predecessor, James, and the mighty Sun King had been busy ruffling other feathers too. Though Ernest Augustus had already made a deal with the Holy Roman Emperor, Louis still hoped that he might be able to turn Hanover to his employer's side. He sent an envoy from the French court to shower the ducal family and the influential Platens with gifts. As William Dutton Colt wryly noted, Ernest Augustus knew how to play the game and 'to show some of us [Ernest Augustus] doth not want money, he bought a jewel of forty thousand crowns from a Jew of Amsterdam, or else it was a present, for by that channel the French money comes.'[3]

Ernest Augustus revelled in being the centre of diplomatic attentions from these two opposing powers, sitting back whilst both sides did all they could to secure his favour. Whilst Duchess Sophia was part-British by birth, Sophia Dorothea was the daughter of a French woman and found herself politically at odds with her mother-in-law and, for the first time, her own father. Though George William had married a French bride, no matter what Ernest Augustus decided, nothing would tempt his brother over to the side of France. George William nursed a great admiration of William III and instead adopted the rather diplomatic approach of attempting to remain neutral. In fact, one might cynically speculate that this attempted neutrality was behind a somewhat timely attack of gout when William III convened a congress of the allies in 1691. Perhaps not, but it was certainly wonderfully convenient for the undecided Duke of Celle!

In the febrile continental atmosphere, William III soon caught wind of the favours that were being bestowed on Hanover by France.

He immediately decided to show the French exactly how one went about lighting up the world stage and as the envoys of these two great powers vied for the favours of Hanover, what had once been a duchy of precious little note was suddenly handed a God-given chance to shine.

The opportunity presented itself during a magnificent festival that was given to welcome the Duke and Duchess of Celle to Hanover. George William and Ernest Augustus were keen to discuss plans for their lands whilst even Sophia and Éléonore managed to give at least the impression of civility. After all, this was a chance for the duchess to show her loathed sister-in-law just how rich and glittering life in Hanover could be. It wasn't only Celle that knew about glamour!

Besides, Duchess Sophia had much to celebrate thanks to events in England and though Ernest Augustus had little interest in her distant chance to become a queen one day, there was nothing he loved so much as an excuse to throw a party. Even better, it gave him the perfect excuse to emulate the Venetian carnivals he had so adored in his homeland of Hanover.

It really was a win all round.

Sophia Dorothea was delighted to have her parents close by again, having found her requests to pay a visit to Celle constantly rebuffed by her husband and his father. They explained that they had better things to spend Hanoverian money on than sending her to Celle with an enormous and expensive retinue, let alone the extravagant gifts that she would be required to take with her but now, Celle was to come to Hanover. The visit was the best of both worlds really, because it meant that the money being spent would at least be enjoyed by the Hanoverian court as well as the party from Celle.

Though George was the official host of festivities, Ernest Augustus and Sophia were the real movers and shakers behind the gathering. The Dukes of Celle and Hanover sat with their spouses on a raised dais and their guests paid homage to them before the party got underway. If ever there was an indication that Hanover was the one to watch, this was it.

To open the celebration, the guests and their hosts enjoyed a play before they processed in state to enjoy a lavish banquet. Once all were fed and watered it was time to get on the dance floor, but Sophia and Éléonore remained seated on the dais, two stately creatures set apart from the dance. How their smiles must have set and stiffened, each no fan of the other's company, and how Éléonore must have loved it, perched there beside the woman who had dismissed her as a *clot of dirt*, the woman who had once made her eat with the servants as the ducal families dined on opulent feasts. Sophia was a realist as much as she was a snob and hosting those she didn't particularly like was all part of the job description. Besides, this was her turf, her rules. Éléonore was an honoured guest, but she would *never* be an electress, let alone a potential queen.

As the two women watched, Sophia Dorothea and her father led the guests in the opening dance of the evening ball, signalling the start to the party in earnest. With his mother keeping her ceremonial place on the dais alongside Éléonore, George squired Clara on the floor, a rather sullen gentleman for such a dazzling and painted lady. We might ask why a mistress was afforded such an honour but in this dance we see precisely why it was that Clara was such a formidable opponent for the young Sophia Dorothea. Yes she was a mistress, the most senior mistress at court and, once the duchess and crown princess were taken out of the equation, the most important of her sex too. Clara knew better than to rely on the vacillations of Ernest Augustus' heart to keep her influence though, and in addition to being a mistress, she was also a wife with clout. Clara's husband, lest we forget, was the prime minister. He sat at Ernest Augustus' right hand and all of that made his spouse a formidably influential woman in her own right. So Clara's dance with George wasn't such a shocker, for she was the most senior female present at the ball once Sophia, Sophia Dorothea and Éléonore were all accounted for.

And at this particular ball, Sophia Dorothea dazzled.

And Königsmarck was more than her match.

The princess was a picture in simple white as Flora, the Roman goddess of spring and flowers. Unlike the heavily made up, dripping-in-bling Clara, Sophia Dorothea wore no jewels and was completely without decoration other than a crown of white flowers in her dark hair. Those lustrous raven locks so beloved of her early biographers could be turned to devastating effect with precious little ornamentation, it seemed, and Sophia Dorothea knew just how to work her best angles.

Putting on a show was something that Königsmarck knew all about and he was resplendent in silver and pink, perfectly complementing Sophia Dorothea. When she finished her dance with Ernest Augustus and her father-in-law passed her to Königsmarck for the next, they were the most splendid sight at the ball.

Clara watched all this with interest and perhaps not a little jealousy. Though it's easy to make Madame von Platen into something of a pantomime villain, all Joan Crawford make up and gnashing teeth, spending her days scheming and plotting and sowing the seeds of mayhem, let's at least give her credit for subtlety. Though Ernest Augustus might have been boorish and ambitious, not to mention crass and insensitive, one doesn't successfully negotiate with the Holy Roman Emperor without more than a little nous and a man with such serious ambitions as Ernest Augustus wouldn't risk them all on a woman who was so monstrous as her rival's biographers have painted her.

Clara, far from being the 'bloated spider' of the most unflattering descriptions, certainly had the ability to charm the best of them. It's easy to look back on the sorry affair of Sophia Dorothea as a melodrama straight out of Hollywood - which brings us back to Joan Crawford - but Clara shouldn't be dismissed as some sort of comically ugly Wicked Witch of the West, slathered in thick greasepaint and crooking one talon-like finger at the men whilst throwing marbles under the feet of the women. She was as ambitious as her husband and lover but unlike them she was a woman and in the world of seventeenth century Hanover, the horizons of even the most go-getting women weren't exactly expansive. As events will show, Clara was far from a misunderstood angel but to dismiss her as a figure of fun or a comic book villainess is to do her a disservice. Like her or loathe her, Clara was the conductor of an orchestra, ensuring everyone stuck to her preferred tempo. A word here, a look there, and Clara von Platen could rule the court.

And she always staked out her territory.

In the centuries since this story took place, what happened next has been presented as absolute proof that Clara was devoted to tormenting Sophia Dorothea. Whether that was the case is a matter for debate, but the events that followed the ball certainly set in motion the chain of misery that followed.

Once he had concluded his dance with Sophia Dorothea and the ball was in full swing, Königsmarck inevitably took the celebrated Clara as his partner. Unlike the young princess, Clara was known to be a willing mistress and a woman whose influence at court was matched only by her appetite for romantic intrigues. Königsmarck was ambitious to climb the ladder of promotion in Hanover and what better way to see his ambitions realised than by winning the favour of the most influential woman at court? He might not have been interested in marrying her daughter, but he was certainly interested in what Clara had to offer.

Though Sophia Dorothea's champions have made great play of Clara's seduction of Königsmarck following his dance with Sophia Dorothea, there should be no doubt that he would have been a more than willing participant. Don't be misled into thinking this was an innocent youth in the hands of a beguiling, painted puppet master. Instead, when Clara invited Königsmarck to accompany her for a private audience at her lavish home of Monplaisir, he was more than keen to accept. She was the most well-connected lady at court, after all, and he was one of the most ambitious gentlemen. Clara wielded power and influence and that, combined with her well-honed charms, was enough to seduce the young count to her bed.

Another notch on the bedpost.

No prizes for guessing what form their *private audience took.*

Yet Königsmarck, as so many do on the morning after, lived to rue his night of passion.

Meeting Melusine

Despite Clara's efforts to bring them back together, Catherine Marie's absence from the bed of George had not made his heart grow fonder. Instead he had simply moved on without her. Although she was now a widow she no longer tempted him as she had during his teens and for now at least, the position of principal mistress to the crown prince remained unfilled.

Anyone at court who had eyes could see that things were not rosy between George and Sophia Dorothea. Since the birth of their children he had notably cooled on her. Although frequently absent on campaigns, even when George was at home the husband and wife barely saw one another. With the first flush of romance gone from the marriage and the children born and squirrelled away with their tutors, what little bloom the couple had enjoyed in the beginning had long since wilted. Now George believed his duty was more or less done. There was an heir even if there was no spare, and he had precious little in common with his crown princess outside of *duty.*

For her part, Sophia Dorothea was just as bored with George as he was with her. She was gregarious and loved the finer things in life whilst he was saturnine and guarded. For a bored young lady with little to fill her days once she had finished strolling in the palace gardens with her mother-in-law, the hours must have passed with a painful slowness. Clara watched all of this with an interested eye but as far as Sophia Dorothea was concerned, there was nothing but friendship between her and her father-in-law's mistresses. Though they weren't close, she little suspected that Clara was about to wield the hammer that would bang the final nail into the coffin of her marriage.

That nail was a tall, skinny lady by the name of Ehrengard Melusine von der Schulenburg[4], known as Melusine. Melusine was the daughter of a noble and was utterly without scandal. Born in 1667, she was single, well-connected and perfectly respectable in every way. She had not been in Hanover long and had been lodged with her father at Clara's Monplaisir residence, so the seasoned mistress had already had plenty of time to get to know her. She presented Melusine to Duchess Sophia as a perfect candidate to serve her as a maid of honour and the duchess happily accepted her into her service. Now we must ask, did Sophia know what Clara was planning for Melusine? It's possible, for she knew Clara well enough to know that there was always an angle, and Sophia was a realist, so she wouldn't have been surprised or upset to find her son with a mistress[5]. In many ways it was better that George chose a candidate who had already been vetted by Clara, because after all, Sophia and Clara's aims were broadly the same, even if their approaches were different. They meant to keep Hanover's star burning brightly and one day both hoped to be sitting at the side of a bona fide *elector*, one as his wife, the other as his mistress.

Melusine was not, it must be said, Clara's equal when it came to scheming. She didn't care too much for manipulation and the accumulation of power, she sought only personal comfort and stability. No doubt under the guidance of the seasoned Clara, Melusine was led to believe that she could expect nothing but luxury if she set her cap at George, so she did just that. Unlike the garrulous Sophia Dorothea, Melusine was far more the equal of George in temperament though let us be kind and say that, if he was sullen, then she was reserved. It sounds better that way!

The lady who became known to the people of England as *the Maypole* met George around 1690 during a break in his military service. The two didn't exactly get on like a house on fire - that wasn't George's style, after all - but they certainly found much to admire in one another. Sophia Dorothea didn't like to ride out and hunt with her husband but Melusine was happy to do both, and whenever George issued an invitation to join him in the saddle, she jumped at it. It's important to give Melusine her due at this point and to say a few words in her defence, because she's all too easy to caricature. If Clara had schemed and climbed ruthlessly over her opponents to reach her position and satisfy her craving for power, Melusine's horizons were far less lofty. At first she was reticent about George's clearly burgeoning attraction and affection for her, for she didn't dislike Sophia Dorothea nor did she have any great desire to cause the crown princess upset. Life at the court of Hanover was expensive though and one thing Melusine didn't have to spare was money. Just as her affair with George William had provided Éléonore with security, and Clara had found a soft cushion thanks to Ernest Augustus, Melusine too could expect her life to become considerably easier if she had the favour of George.

Melusine offered a few charms of her own too. Her father, Gustavus Adolphus, Baron von der Schulenburg, served as Privy Councillor to the Elector of Brandenburg whilst her brother, Johann Matthias, stood on the brink of a long and glittering military career. Just as becoming mistress to George would lend Melusine a new power at the Hanoverian court, so too would she bring potentially vital empire-building connections to Ernest Augustus and his son. They needed them too, as the row over primogeniture had created a hell of a stink in Hanover and even before two sons had met their deaths, the atmosphere was far from jolly. Yet feuding was all set aside by Ernest Augustus in his fevered desire to see his lands raised to an electorate and if Melusine delivered him the ear of the Elector of Brandenburg, then he could see nothing but perfection in the woman who had caught his son's wandering eye. Years later, her status cemented and her title now that of Duchess of Kendal, Melusine had risen to a pinnacle of importance that Sophia Dorothea never came close to. Even the king of France, Louis XV, wrote of her to Count Broglio, "THERE is no room to doubt, that the Duchess of Kendal, having a great ascendance over the king of Great Britain, and maintaining a strict union with his ministers, must materially influence their principal resolutions. You will neglect nothing to acquire a share of her confidence."[6]

Sophia Dorothea would never be discussed in such august terms.

Soon George and Melusine were inseparable and Sophia Dorothea could only watch as the lady who had seemingly come out of nowhere gradually usurped her place at the side of George. The increasingly isolated Sophia Dorothea began to believe that Clara was a friend to be trusted and Clara, in turn, took every opportunity to make innocent mention of the places in which George and Melusine had been seen together. Whether hunting, enjoying the opera or attending the theatre, she dropped these little nuggets into their conversations, ably planting the seeds that would undermine Sophia Dorothea's confidence at court even further. At the same time, she and her husband were contriving to arrange gatherings at which Melusine and the crown prince could enjoy one another's company.

Clara was a masterful choreographer.

Catherine Marie, widowed and in search of a new escort now George had rejected her, was not to stay single forever. Not long after her return to Hanover she became betrothed to a general in the Hanoverian army, and Clara was determined to mark her sister's latest triumph with a glittering wedding party. Never a lady who did things by halves, Clara decided that it would be a party for the ages and though she knew that Melusine and George intended to attend together and make their attachment public, protocol dictated that Sophia Dorothea should also receive an invitation. Clara didn't want to rely on Sophia Dorothea's sense of duty to ensure that she attended though so under her usual cover of friendship, she encouraged the crown princess to put on her glad rags and join the dancing.

And see her husband consorting with his mistress too.

Sophia Dorothea, little suspecting how masterfully she was being manipulated, rsvp'd in the affirmative, promising that she would come to the wedding party. Though she didn't know it, humiliation would be waiting for her. Yet as the wedding wore on and the dancing began, she didn't appear. George and Melusine took their place hand in hand on the dance floor but of Sophia Dorothea, there remained no sign. Clara did all she could to ensure that George and Melusine delayed their first public dance until Sophia Dorothea could arrive but ultimately she found her efforts defeated. Later in the evening Sophia Dorothea finally sent her apologies. She had been taken ill, she explained, and was sorry to have missed the celebrations.

Everyone who had *not* missed the party, however, now knew beyond a doubt that Melusine and George were an item and though she thought that her plan had failed, Clara was to discover that was far from the case. The letter of apology sent by Sophia Dorothea had been personally delivered by Knesebeck, Sophia Dorothea's friend and confidante. As luck would have it, she had arrived at precisely the moment that George and his newly-minted mistress took the floor and when she returned to Sophia Dorothea, she carried with her an outraged account of all that she had seen.

The impact of George's very public display of affection for Melusine really cannot be underestimated. Mistresses were a part of life for the vast majority of royal wives but there was generally an unspoken understanding when it came to the crunch. With so many marriages contracted not for love but for business and dynasty, innumerable wives agreed to be complicit in their husband's *amours* on the understanding that they wouldn't suffer any detriment or embarrassment as a result. George had flouted both of these rules. Since the birth of her daughter and for much of the period of her pregnancy, Sophia Dorothea had been at best tolerated and at worst ignored. George wasn't expected to be a doting and ever-present husband but at the very least he should have given the impression that he respected his wife. That impression was, as everyone could see, distinctly lacking.

Dancing with one's mistress at an official occasion wasn't particularly scandalous but Sophia Dorothea's absence gave a whole new weight to the matter. Added to this, Clara was sure to make the couple's dance as public as possible and they were even awarded more precedence than the bride and groom themselves. It was a public humiliation for Sophia Dorothea and it was entirely intentional. She was expected to learn her place and learn it well.

'Look at that tall mawkin, and think of her being my son's passion,' Duchess Sophia crowed, and they certainly made an odd couple. As taciturn as each other, though Melusine was of an even temper whereas George's was fiery, she stood a head and shoulders taller than him and was of such extravagant height that it was impossible for her to fade into the background. Despite her imposing figure Melusine was far from showy and she was no ambitious professional mistress after the fashion of the estimable Clara.

None of this stopped Count von Königsmarck from firing a shot across George's bow. Never without a tale to tell, Königsmarck loved to regale his audience with his wit and storytelling, throwing in gossip and scandal as he went. It was whilst entertaining one evening that he dared to take a swipe at George. He was in the middle of a tale about the delights and splendour of the Dresden court, at the centre of the Electorate of Saxony, when George decided that he had had enough. If Dresden was so magnificent, he asked, why didn't Königsmarck just go back there? Königsmarck's reply was withering. He told George, 'Because I could not bear to see a prince destroy the life and happiness of his good and beautiful wife by neglecting her for an impudent and worthless mistress!'[7]

Did somebody say Melusine?

One can only imagine the shocked silence that must have fallen over the assembled courtiers. Though marital relations in Dresden weren't exactly rosy, everyone knew exactly what Königsmarck was really getting at and just who the 'beautiful wife' and 'worthless mistress' were. George let the moment pass, but it must have done little for his love of this showy charmer who seemed to have won virtually everybody over to his cause.

History, like Königsmarck, has not been kind to Melusine. 'The taste exhibited by the prince, in the selection of his mistresses, was outrageously bad,'[8] wrote one commentator, considering her 'destitute of charms' and a creature of unfathomable appeal to anyone. In fact she was pretty inoffensive and though she later made a monumental misstep when she advised George, by then King George I, to support the initiative that led to the popping of the South Sea Bubble[9], she was fairly blameless too. It was Clara who had a talent for trouble. Melusine had no axe to grind against Sophia Dorothea. All she wanted was an easy life. Sophia Dorothea, however, had come from a court where mistresses weren't the done thing. Her parents had married for love and she expected no less than that from her own spouse. Tired of being pushed aside in favour of Melusine, Sophia Dorothea went to George and asked what she might do to win him back as a friend at least, if not more.

George, taciturn and bad-tempered, refused to discuss the matter but Sophia Dorothea, showing some of her mother's tenacity, refused to be silenced. The outcome was an explosion of anger on both sides and as Sophia Dorothea ranted, George violently attacked his wife. He threw her to the ground and tried to throttle her before her attendants intervened, bundling a shell shocked Sophia Dorothea from the room and out of danger. She was so upset that she took to her bed and refused to receive any visitors, not that her husband tried to make contact anyway.

With Sophia Dorothea in despair and George utterly furious, the court became a suddenly very small, seething place. Though some have accused Duchess Sophia of being a wicked mother-in-law with nothing but the torment of her husband's wife to entertain her, this is a far from fair assessment of her character. She wasn't cruel, nor did she revel in Sophia Dorothea's misery, but she certainly *was* a realist. Sophia Dorothea and George were married and that wasn't about to change, so they would have to learn to live together in something resembling peace - if not that, at least mutual ambivalence.

Fearing a scandal, Sophia decided that a change of air would do everybody good, as she often did at moments of crisis. She packed up her daughter-in-law and grandchildren and took them off to her personal sanctuary at Herrenhausen, where they could breathe fresh air and escape the trouble at home. Sophia loved Herrenhausen and was never happier than when she was strolling in the gardens, away from the politicking of Hanover, so it's perfectly possible that she hoped Sophia Dorothea would find the place as peaceful as she did. When she returned, Sophia Dorothea found that George had been given a telling off and for a short time at least, he managed to be civil to his wife.

It didn't last.

Escaping Clara's Clutches

In bedding the young, popular, and ridiculously dashing Königsmarck, Clara had succeeded admirably in winning quite the victory over her imagined rival, Sophia Dorothea. When her parents returned to Celle after a visit, the young wife found herself alone again and Königsmarck, her childhood friend, was now occupied with his new, experienced mistress. Sophia Dorothea was a woman of strong emotions and they were rarely governed, so we can imagine the no doubt dramatic scenes when she and Königsmarck enjoyed their first meeting after his capitulation to Clara.

Königsmarck wanted a night of uncomplicated passion but uncomplicated wasn't in Clara's vocabulary and he soon realised that he had made a mistake. The count was an adventurer. He was a young man who enjoyed the dashing life he had carved out for himself and he didn't want to become the pet of an older woman, yet he had succeeded in becoming just that, and Clara clung onto Königsmarck for all she was worth.

On the one hand assuring Sophia Dorothea that he was still the closest ally she had at the isolated court whilst on the other keeping Clara sweet, Königsmarck was playing two incompatible roles. Worse still, he was all too aware that should any suggestion of his intimacy with Clara reach the ears of Ernest Augustus, there would be trouble. As naive when it came to his mistress as he was worldly when it came to politics, Ernest Augustus honestly believed that Clara was faithful to him alone. Should he learn that Königsmarck had been her lover, the young count's stratospheric rise through the ranks in Hanover would be cut unceremoniously short and Clara would sashay on without censure. She held Ernest Augustus in her palm and need only to paint herself as the unwilling object of Königsmarck's unwanted advances to earn the continued adoration of her long term lover. Likewise, should Königsmarck attempt to break off their affair then she might do that anyway, telling Ernest Augustus that the younger man had attempted to compromise her. Whatever the outcome, it could only end unhappily for Königsmarck.

There can be few more damning ways of ending a relationship than to elect to go into battle rather than remain in the bedroom, but that's exactly what Königsmarck did. Rather than face the wrath of Clara and Ernest Augustus, he chose instead to volunteer to serve with the Hanoverian forces. It was a crucial time as the French, losing their grip on the occupied Palatinate homelands of George's mother, adopted a slash and burn policy across the land that they had been unable to secure. It was to join the armies of the Grand Alliance in the Palatinate that Königsmarck was sent, far away from Clara and rather less happily away from Sophia Dorothea.

Safely out of the way of romance on the Rhine, the young soldier did his bit for his adopted home whilst in Hanover, life was not quite as cheery as once it had been. With fighting continuing both in the Palatinate and the Balkans, where the armies of the Holy Roman Empire were battling the Turks, the coffers of Hanover were stretched. At the court the parties continued but in the land around the palaces, life was bleak for the poor. Life was just as bleak on the two warring fronts, and Sophia Dorothea had lost not only the friendship of Königsmarck but of her favourite brother-in-law, Charles Philip, too.

Charles Philip was lost whilst fighting in the Morea and for a time, his fate was unknown. His fellow soldiers had been routed and of the thousands who set out, less than 150 returned. Still the ducal family prayed that their son would be amongst them.

At home, Charles Philip's parents were in torment as they waited for news and on 18 February 1690 it seemed as though they would soon learn of his fate. Sir William Dutton Colt, King William's envoy at the court of Hanover, wrote to civil servant Richard Warre that, 'The last letters from Vienna say positively that Prince Charles is taken and carried to Constantinople; the news comes from several prisoners that have ransoms, one of whom was a captain under the Prince, but none of them saw him a prisoner, but they were told by the Turks that they had given 200,000 dollars to the Tartars for him. The Duke and Duchess are much comforted.'[10]

Three days later Colt was reporting that he had been shown letters from a captain who had seen and spoken to the missing prince. It was a lifeline at last. The court readied itself to negotiate the ransom that would see Charles Philip granted his freedom and Duchess Sophia, beside herself with worry, finally allowed herself to be comforted by the news that he might soon be home. Sadly, the comfort provided by such reports soon proved to be nothing more than false hope. Colt's dispatch of 25 February reported that the realities of war had made themselves jarringly apparent to the duke and duchess in Hanover.

> 'We have received certain news that Prince Charles was killed on the spot where his body was found, with several of his officers and servants round him. This has increased our sorrow here.'[11]

Charles Philip, Duchess Sophia's favourite son, was dead. His mother was plunged into a deep depression that left those around her fearing for her life and the family closed ranks, mourning its lost son. Éléonore and George William travelled to Hanover from Celle and the ducal brothers, at odds over matters of power and territory, found themselves united by shared grief. Yet Charles Philip wasn't the only man away fighting, and for Sophia Dorothea and Clara, both eagerly awaiting news of their favourite soldier on the Rhine, there was a worrying lack of news.

This time fate smiled on the unfortunate court and Königsmarck returned from his military escapades to the place where he had caused such a stir. If Königsmarck had hoped to create some distance between himself and Clara, front line service had done just that. On his return he made no effort to officially end his affair with the countess, but simply no longer visited her chambers for amorous adventures. Instead he spent time with the grieving Sophia Dorothea, a much needed friend when her husband was as distant as ever. In fact, George wasn't only emotionally distant but soon geographically too. He departed for Flanders leaving Königsmarck at home in Hanover, if only temporarily.

The fate of Charles Philip played on Königsmarck's mind. He and the young man had been friends and Charles Philip's presence had been the perfect excuse for Königsmarck to pay visits to Sophia Dorothea. Under cover of seeing her brother-in-law he had stolen a few moments with her but now, with Charles Philip gone, so too was his alibi. If Clara had been fooled before - and Clara saw *everything* - she wouldn't be fooled again.

Though Königsmarck no longer visited the countess to partake of her favours he remained a regular caller at Sophia Dorothea's chambers, this time accompanied by his very handy sister, and Clara seethed over it. Her rival enjoyed the favour of Ernest Augustus even if George found her objectionable, so there was little to be gained in reporting the meetings to him. All Sophia Dorothea's indulgent father-in-law would do was dismiss her follies as harmless intrigues and Clara could hardly risk him becoming suspicious of her own affair with Königsmarck. All she could do was what she did best. That was gather intelligence, scheme, and wait for the moment to strike.

When Königsmarck received word that he was soon to return to the front, he finally told the crown princess that his feelings had progressed beyond friendship. No doubt she was flattered, for Sophia Dorothea, a celebrated beauty and once the centre of her adoring parents' universe, had long since become part of the furniture for George. He was happy with Melusine and his wife was nothing more than an unwanted distraction. What Sophia Dorothea wasn't, however, was an easy conquest. She lacked Clara's experience in matters of seduction but seduction had never been particularly necessary for Sophia Dorothea. Her mother had raised her as a princess, with all the attendant sense of self worth that such an upbringing included. She wanted to be wooed.

Sophia Dorothea was not about to tumble into bed with her soldier but she graciously gave him permission to write to her whilst he was away in Flanders. This may at first glance appear to be innocent but if that was the case, then why did Sophia Dorothea specify that he must address his letters not to her, but to her closest friend and attendant, Eleonore von dem Knesebeck? The implication is all too clear: both Sophia Dorothea and Königsmarck were implicitly acknowledging that the content of the letters might not be so innocent. The intention behind them *certainly* wasn't innocent and Königsmarck's language even at this early stage was like that of a lovesick youth.

Sadly, many of the letters sent by Sophia Dorothea no longer exist, but we must imagine from the florid content of those from Königsmarck that he was replying in kind. As early as June 1690, his tone was already far beyond that of friendship and his efforts to capture the young woman's heart had, it seems, already begun.

> 'I have reached the end; and the only thing which can still save me is a few lines written in your own incomparable hand. If I were fortunate enough to hear from you I would be comforted. I hope you will have the charity not to deny me this favour, as it is you who are the cause of my suffering, it is only right that you should be the one to take it away. Only you can soothe the deadly pain I feel at being away from you, and only then shall I know if I could really believe the kind words you had said to me once or twice. If I were not writing to someone for whom my respect is as great as my love, I would find better words to express my feelings; but fearing to offend, I will end here, begging you to think of me sometimes and believe me your slave.'

It is particularly telling that he asked her to reply in her own hand, not to dictate her response to her friend. Königsmarck wanted the rejection to come from Sophia Dorothea with no involvement from intermediaries at all but whatever her response might have said, it certainly wasn't the rejection he had challenged her to send! Instead the next letter celebrated their reunion and begged her once again, as Königsmarck always did, to be true in her affections.

For a man like Königsmarck, a romantic, dashing adventurer, this in itself shouldn't be taken as proof of a sexual affair. What it was, however, was proof of a relationship that had already stepped beyond the boundaries of what was acceptable and with Sophia Dorothea's marriage to George by now little more than a war of attrition, it's no wonder that the unhappy woman was drawn in by her keen, charming suitor.

Though things were back on track for a day or two at least, it didn't last. It never lasted. Soon the words were flying from Königsmarck's pen at an alarming rate, begging for a word, for a crumb of comfort, and apparently receiving nothing in return. It's clear that Sophia Dorothea didn't reply and Königsmarck's letters became increasingly desperate until, finally, she deigned to respond to his pleas. What exactly was said we have no way of knowing but Königsmarck assured his paramour that he understood she must take care and that he must do likewise. Clearly the 'sweetest, loveliest person in the world,' as he termed her, had warned her suitor of the danger of discovery. Let us not forget that George had already assaulted his wife and though Königsmarck was away and relatively safe from punishment, Sophia Dorothea had no such buffer between her and her husband.

When Königsmarck returned to Hanover he didn't find an adoring albeit married woman waiting to throw her arms around him but a guarded wife, who was all too aware of the possible consequences of inappropriate behaviour occurring under the very noses of her husband's family. She behaved with utmost propriety and refused to see Königsmarck alone, creating an impenetrable shield of ladies-in-waiting and attendants around her to preserve her virtue. In fact, all of this ended up going just a little too far and Königsmarck, always a spirited and melodramatic correspondent, went into overdrive.

How could she do this to him, he cried, fairly beating his literary breast, to the man who adored her, who was desperate to talk to her and who would die from the pain of being kept apart? 'When I think I shall not be seeing you for a whole week,' wrote Königsmarck, by now in his mid-twenties, 'I feel so desperate I want to plunge a dagger in my heart. But since I must live, I beg you to let me live always for you.'

If it seems a little melodramatic, that's because it was. Sophia Dorothea, however, would not be persuaded. She maintained her steely determination to remain detached and for all his desperate pleas, nothing Königsmarck could say would move her.

For now.

And all the time, Clara was watching.

The Diplomatic Stage

Whilst all of this intriguing was going on in Hanover, on the world stage matters were just as fiery, if considerably less intimate. In January 1691, a year after the death of Charles Philip, William III called his fellow leaders to The Hague, where he intended to convene a congress of the allies to decide on the next moves in the Nine Years' War.

And he did it in style.

> '[William III] hoped that his kind fellow townsmen would consider him as a neighbour, born and bred among them, and would not pay him so bad a compliment as to treat him ceremoniously. But all his expostulations were vain. The Hollanders, simple and parsimonious as their ordinary habits were, had set their hearts on giving their illustrious countryman a reception suited to his dignity and to his merit; and he found it necessary to yield. On the day of his triumph the concourse was immense. All the wheeled carriages and horses of the province were too few for the multitude of those who flocked to the show. Many thousands came sliding or skating along the frozen canals from Amsterdam, Rotterdam, Leyden, Haarlem, Delft. At ten in the morning of the twenty sixth of January, the great bell of the Town House gave the signal. Sixteen hundred substantial burghers, well-armed, and clad in the finest dresses which were to be found in the recesses of their wardrobes, kept order in the crowded streets. Balconies and scaffolds, embowered in evergreens and hung with tapestry, hid the windows. The royal coach, escorted by an army of halberdiers and running footmen, and followed by a long train of splendid equipages passed, under numerous arches rich with carving and painting, amidst incessant shouts of "Long live the King our Stadtholder."[12]

And of course, when the King of England called, his allies were sure to follow. As William once again settled into his ancestral lands he was joined for the vital talks by Frederick, Elector of Brandenburg, who a few years later took the title of King in Prussia. 'Then arrived the young

Elector of Bavaria, the Regent of Wirtemberg [sic], the Landgraves of Hesse Cassel and Hesse Darmstadt, and a long train of sovereign princes sprung from the illustrious houses of Brunswick, of Saxony, of Holstein, and of Nassau. The Marquess of Gastanaga, Governor of the Spanish Netherlands, repaired to the assembly from the viceregal Court of Brussels. Extraordinary ministers had been sent by the Emperor, by the Kings of Spain, Poland, Denmark, and Sweden and by the Duke of Savoy.'[13]

With these illustrious names came vast numbers of officials and fashionable hangers-on, desperate to be at the centre of the action. For those who already held influence the congress was an invitation not to be ignored, whilst for those who sought to increase their standing there was no better place in Europe to be seen. Alongside Ernest Augustus came his eldest son and heir, George, and at his side was Sophia Dorothea, no doubt delighted to be taking a break from the stultifying atmosphere at home. Also in the party from Hanover were the omnipresent Platens and Count von Königsmarck, making up what must have surely been a rather awkward travelling group. Of George William there was no sign. Sophia Dorothea's father, torn between his loyalties to his French wife and his English sister-in-law, had been struck down by a convenient attack of gout. For a man who would literally travel across countries to attend a party this was quite a thing, and he asked his brother to represent him in his absence. Of course, Ernest Augustus was happy to comply.

The Hague fairly shimmered with the opulence and brilliance on display and whilst talks continued during the day, in the evening the only thing on the agenda was fun. The theatres were packed and the gaming tables crowded, whilst those with money to splash around held magnificent banquets and parties, all designed to win new friends and outdo their peers. Though the congress was intended to discuss the best way to put a stop to the ceaseless march of the armies of Louis XIV, it was also an excellent opportunity to show off.

The discussions were delicate and protracted and with so many heads of state involved, they were bound to drag on. Whilst the sheer size of the alliance was a guarantee of military might, it was also a guarantee of warring egos. Here were more than a dozen nations, each bringing with them their own history and ambitions, their own disputes and alliances, and William intended to steer them into something resembling a harmonious agreement. Under debate was how many troops each country would contribute to make up the intended total of 220,000 men, but it was a delicate discussion, taking two steps back for every step forward. Louis XIV had no such difficulty for he had no vast alliance to marshal, no monarchs and their envoys to negotiate into submission.

As the Grand Alliance in The Hague carved up their military responsibilities, Louis XIV was planning what would prove to be a decisive move. In March 1691 the armies of France made an assault on Mons and besieged the city. Situated in the Spanish-Netherlands, Mons was a strategically vital location and the French forces easily secured the victory, taking minimal losses. For the members of the Grand Alliance it was a ringing blow, and one that wasn't easily forgotten. For Sophia Dorothea and Königsmarck, the trip to The Hague seemed to be a watershed of a rather different sort.

In such close quarters to her husband and Königsmarck, who was still nothing more compromising than a friend, Sophia Dorothea behaved impeccably. She made a rare decision not to opt for the dramatic and held her would-be suitor at arm's length. Perhaps she was aware of Clara's jealous attentions; perhaps she was afraid to progress things further, caught between her duty as respectable courtly wife and her desire as a neglected, lonely woman. Whatever it was, for now at least there was nothing more scandalous happening than the usual overdose of gossip and meaningful glances.

Despite the stakes that were under discussion at the congress of the allies, The Hague revelled in its status as the hottest ticket on the continent. As the city bulged at the seams with the sheer number of fashionable, illustrious visitors, Königsmarck was in his element. Always on the lookout for the next opportunity to increase his own fortunes, he was utterly star struck when he met William III and the king in turn was impressed by his dashing new acquaintance.

Perhaps tired of being nothing more than a good friend to Sophia Dorothea, Königsmarck left The Hague, but he did not to go home to Hanover. Instead he went off to temporarily serve with the English army. Why he did this remains a mystery but he never missed a chance to curry favour and adventuring was in his blood, so it was likely just one of the soldier's many ambitious whims. Whatever was behind it, Königsmarck soon changed his mind and headed back to Hanover and the start of what would prove to be a deadly affair.

Codes, Gloves and Cunning

Precisely when Sophia Dorothea and Königsmarck segued from friendship into romance is a matter of conjecture; we cannot be sure and their always florid letters offer no concrete proof. In fact, even before they appear to have been intimate, Königsmarck's correspondence was couched in the same heated terms of those written at the height of the affair, but following the trip to The Hague and his brief departure to join the English, it appears as though Sophia Dorothea gave up her efforts to keep him at a safe distance. Perhaps it was the death of Charles Philip that did it, serving as a timely reminder of the risks he was facing every day that he was away from home. Perhaps it was the ease of the French victory at Mons, signalling an escalation in hostilities, or perhaps it was simply the wide public knowledge of her husband's own love affair with his *tall mawkin*, Melusine. Whatever tipped the balance, by the summer of 1691 our risky lovers were very definitely testing the limits of what could be termed *platonic*.

And how subtly the changes came, as the valediction that had once declared Königsmarck Sophia Dorothea's *faithful servant* became the far more intimate, 'farewell my beloved brunette, I kiss your knees.'

In a world of cyphers and codes, of hidden letters and clandestine meetings in locations referred to only as 'you know where', the ways of determining affection were many. For Sophia Dorothea and Königsmarck, one of them was the wax seal that the soldier used to close his letters. At first the seal was the image of a flaming heart upon an altar, illuminated by a bright sun. Accompanying the image was the motto, 'rien impure inallurne', which translates as 'nothing impure can set me on fire'.

Nothing impure?

Every eyebrow in Hanover must have been raised when they heard *that*.

Königsmarck was known as a dashing cavalier, a gallant with a love of the finer things in life and a fellow who was experienced in the ways of romance. Sophia Dorothea, on the other hand, had seen little of life beyond palace walls. She had gone from spoiled child to neglected wife in the blink of an eye and a man like Königsmarck must have been tempting indeed. He didn't only offer the promise of romance of course, but he was also a physical link back to the early days in Celle, when the carefree princess had gallivanted with the young soldier-in-training in the grounds of her home. To have that palpable reminder of happier days so close must have been a tonic for Sophia Dorothea now she lived in Hanover, in a court she had never warmed to. Königsmarck offered friendship and devotion, and he reminded her of this at every turn. His letters, impassioned and florid, promised constancy and adoration and assured her that, 'I have forsworn all other women for you; if you doubt this, name any one you would like me to abandon, and I will never speak to her again.'

Mindful of the danger of discovery, Sophia Dorothea did all she could to conceal the existence of the letters from her husband and his confidantes. She and Königsmarck used both his sister, Aurora, and Sophia Dorothea's attendant, Eleonore von dem Knesebeck, as their go-betweens. The letters were left in prearranged drop spots such as hats and gloves and were concealed in the lining of curtains or any secret nook or cranny that Sophia Dorothea could find. How thrilled she must have been to be the centre of attention once more, to no longer be stagnating in the court she had never wanted to join anyway. In childhood Sophia Dorothea's parents had told her that she was beautiful and special, a girl in a million, but her husband had no such illusions. Count von Königsmarck, however, knew exactly how to flatter. Sophia Dorothea was a girl again, living in a world of intrigue and romance and for the first time in years, she was the apple of someone's eye.

And she had displaced Clara, who had once seemed unassailable.

All of this couldn't pass without notice in the intense Hanover court, where men and women revelled in the gossip and drama of day to day life.

And Königsmarck was a constant fount of both.

When it came to this Don Juan's letters to Sophia Dorothea, that chivalrous seal, needless to say, didn't last. Lest his amorous motive be misunderstood - which frankly seems unlikely - Königsmarck changed his seal for another and this one carried a rather different sort of meaning. The altar and sunlight were gone and in their place was a heart enclosed inside another. Gone was any mention of *impure* and instead the seal bore the motto, 'cosi fosse il vostro dentro il mio.'

And what, you ask, does this mean? In fact, it translates as 'thus might yours be inside mine,' which one can only hope refers to nothing more saucy than those intertwined hearts. Of course there are other ways to interpret it, but however we choose to read his meaning, it is one of affection, not innocence.

And for a woman like Clara, where there was forbidden affection to be discovered, there was mischief to be made.

When George returned to Hanover from Flanders he no doubt remembered the explosion of temper that had ended in his attempted strangulation of his wife and her hurried departure for the sanctuary of Herrenhausen. His mother had told her son in no uncertain terms that such behaviour couldn't be repeated and he grudgingly did his best to at least appear attentive, though it was an effort that didn't last. As part of this attempted truce, when George returned from Flanders in 1691, he brought with him a gift for his wife in the form of a pair of beautifully embroidered gloves.

Königsmarck was also home from his latest adventures and as befit one of the most glittering men at court, he marked his safe return with a magnificent masked ball. Clara saw her chance to create some real trouble for the woman who she believed had stolen her young lover away and contrived to somehow steal one of the gloves that George had brought his wife on his return from Flanders. Sophia Dorothea was too preoccupied to notice it was missing but it would turn up again soon enough, in somewhat compromising circumstances.

Safely behind her mask, Clara deftly caught the attention at Königsmarck during the ball and the passionate, arrogant and rather easily led young man allowed himself to be tempted away from the party by the seemingly unknown lady. He followed her out into the secluded grounds and into a pavilion, where the two might be unobserved. Little did the foolish Königsmarck know that Clara and her husband had planned all of this with military precision. Clara had no weapons to hand though, just the stolen glove that was concealed against her celebrated bosom.

Count von Platen had been given strict instructions by his wife of what exactly he should do and when, and he followed them to the letter. George was never the sort of chap who enjoyed parties so it was easy for the politician to engage him in conversation and with the noisy, lively ball in full swing, it was no challenge for Platen to convince George to stroll in the gardens with him, away from the crowded ballroom.

Together the two men ambled through the grounds towards the pavilion where Clara and Königsmarck were enjoying each other's company. Clara remained alert to every movement outside and hearing her husband approaching as arranged, she accidentally-on-purpose dropped the stolen glove and fled the scene, leaving Königsmarck resolutely unfulfilled. Platen pantomimed innocence as to the identity of the woman and the importance of the glove, which he retrieved and presented to George as a token of the interrupted interlude. No doubt George found the sight of the seemingly embarrassed woman fleeing the scene of the seduction amusing, but his amusement lasted precisely as long as it took him to see the glove that the woman had dropped.

George would certainly have recognised the lavish gift he had brought with him from Flanders for his wife but there in the pavilion, faced with what appeared to be proof of her betrayal, he said nothing. He didn't need to, for Clara and her husband knew that their plan had been successful. George believed that his own wife had been in that hidden pavilion with Count von Königsmarck and from that moment on, any chance of reconciliation - slight though it was - crashed and burned.

As 1691 wore on, Königsmarck and Sophia Dorothea continued their clandestine correspondence and their burgeoning affair. But Sophia Dorothea seemed to grow timid once again and fearing detection, attempted to distance herself from her lover. Coming so soon after Clara's pantomime with that embroidered glove one can only wonder if George had approached his wife and asked her what had become of the gifts he brought her from Flanders. If so, she would have no answer for him. Any question about the gloves would have caught Sophia Dorothea on the back foot completely, unable to produce the missing garment but equally unable to account for its loss.

After all, only the mysterious masked woman caught in the pavilion rendezvous could answer to that.

But if George wasn't a dutiful husband, nor was he a fan of Clara. He knew the court well enough to know that only one woman was capable of choreographing the sort of scene that he had so conveniently happened upon in the grounds and he was far too wily to think that Count von Platen's invitation to stroll beside the pavilion was a coincidence. What George probably didn't suspect was that Clara was the woman in the tryst. He more likely believed that he *had* caught Sophia Dorothea and Königsmarck together, but he would no doubt have sensed Clara's involvement in the discovery. If Clara expected her efforts to provoke the mother of all drama she was mistaken, as George had no wish to dance to the tune she had tried to conduct. Instead, the incident seemingly passed unremarked.

George wasn't the only jealous man in Sophia Dorothea's life though. Königsmarck was equally as possessive of his paramour as her husband. Ironic, given that George had no love for his wife, busy as he was with Melusine. Whether he paid her any heed or not Sophia Dorothea was George's wife. The very idea that she would dare to ape him and take a lover of her own would have been enough to throw him into another of those terrible rages of his.

Königsmarck, meanwhile, was in despair at the lack of time he was able to spend with Sophia Dorothea, but he had a plan. He took a house on the edge of the palace estates in Hanover. The property could be accessed directly from the gardens where Sophia Dorothea took her exercise and after dark, she could easily have passed unnoticed into his home.

Sophia Dorothea frequently dictated her letters to Knesebeck and she delivered them on her mistress' behalf to Königsmarck, Aurora, or a member of Königsmarck's household. In some cases Königsmarck even wrote his replies as though they were intended for the confidante rather than her married friend. Should the letters have fallen into the wrong hands, the fact that they were written by Sophia Dorothea's friend would have provided some measure of protection but it was a veneer of safety at best and without the help of her trusted lady in waiting, the affair between Königsmarck and Sophia Dorothea would have been much more difficult to conceal. It was she who stood guard as they enjoyed their intimate liaisons and she alone who Sophia Dorothea entrusted with knowledge of the affair.

In public the couple's meetings were brief, *too* brief perhaps, and liable to arouse suspicion for that very reason, but whatever occurred in public, it made the always melodramatic Königsmarck even more fevered. For her part, Sophia Dorothea tormented herself with thoughts of the other women he had known and still, she suspected, consorted with. She pushed him away and pulled him closer and he fed the fire with endless protestations and breast-beating proclamations of love in letters which could never have been passed off as platonic.

> 'How could you possibly think I could love anyone but you? No, I protest that after you I shall never love again. It will not be difficult to keep my word, for once I have loved you, I can find no other woman pretty. You wrong yourself if you think such a thing. How can you compare yourself with

others? And how could it be possible, after I have loved a goddess, to look at mortals? [...] I adore you, dark charmer, and I shall die with these feelings in my heart. If you do not forget me, I swear to you that I shall love you as long as I live.'

Königsmarck fell ill with a fever in 1691 and found himself with plenty of time on his hands to write, as well as plenty of time to receive visitors. He begged Sophia Dorothea to call and see him and with Aurora staying at his home, the couple found themselves with the perfect alibi and a ready-made, entirely complicit chaperone who could preserve the illusion of respectability. He warned Sophia Dorothea that her absence, as well as a lack of letters, was serving only to make his sickness worse and just as Königsmarck knew she would, Sophia Dorothea jumped to answer his demands.

Her answer was far from what Königsmarck had been expecting. Rather than rush to the side of his sickbed, the conflicted Sophia Dorothea suggested that it might be better for everyone concerned if he left Hanover altogether. He replied to tell her that he would obey since, 'if I could just die quietly somewhere I would be happy.' Of course Königsmarck wasn't dying but he was never a man who knowingly downplayed a situation. Even so, he wasn't without offers elsewhere, both personal and professional, and for all his purple prose, the situation in which he had found himself was hardly enviable.

Sophia Dorothea and Königsmarck were a heady mix and well-suited in terms of drama, but in their moments of clarity both must have seen the hopelessness of their situation. Königsmarck was a respected soldier across the continent and one can imagine that it must have seemed tempting to return to his native land of Sweden, where his family had known such success. In Hanover he was the gallant, embroiled in an affair that constantly jumped between declarations of love and orders of dismissal, but if he were to answer the call of his homeland he might forget Sophia Dorothea and concentrate instead on the military world in which his family was so distinguished. If he had done so our story might have had a happier ending, but he didn't. He resolved to remain in Hanover, a place that was on the verge of becoming an electorate, where Ernest Augustus might promise those in his service opportunities to advance and win influence. Hanover was also the land where Königsmarck enjoyed taking centre stage - a massive and much sought after fish in a rather small court. And he loved the attention that it brought him.

Königsmarck's exultations of death startled Sophia Dorothea and she took the bait, apparently making one of her secret visits to see her ailing lover. To seal their commitment, Königsmarck made what he considered the ultimate gesture of devotion and assured his lover that his letters were signed in blood. Given his love of the overly dramatic gesture, he might even have been telling the truth.

The Companionate Bear

Ernest Augustus had a nose for politics. He could sniff out a deal from a thousand paces and he knew exactly how to turn the screws to ensure that he got what he wanted, from primogeniture to the Grand Alliance and all the way to his very own electoral cap. In this, he and his wife were perfectly suited. After all, hadn't Sophia had shown more than a little political nous of her own when she had convinced George William to pledge his daughter's hand to George instead of the son of Duke Anthony Ulrich of Wolfenbüttel? In his own wife, Éléonore Desmier d'Olbreuse, George William had married a similarly ambitious, intelligent woman but for his part, ambition was something that seemed to fade as the years passed.

George William was content to let his brother be the man who revelled in political intrigue whilst he, convenient attacks of gout allowing, lived the life of a country gentleman at home in Celle. Every year as the autumn leaves turned russet on the bough he travelled to his country seat at Epsdorff and indulged himself in a spot of hunting, all the better to escape the noise and glitter of the Celle court. In the past he had been accompanied only by his wife but in 1691 he decided to make it a larger affair. George William invited Ernest Augustus and his family to join him on his trip and Ernest Augustus gladly accepted. Also on the invite list was Duke Anthony Ulrich and the three men thought that the jaunt might give them the perfect opportunity to hold their very own miniature summit. Whilst their days would be spent riding out in the autumn sun, once evening fell the three men would discuss more weighty matters, such as where their loyalties lay in regard to France and the Grand Alliance. It was the perfect mix of work and play.

As George's wife, Sophia Dorothea was naturally expected to join the party but for Königsmarck, there was to be no hunting. Instead, Ernest Augustus asked the Swede to travel to Hamburg, some eight miles away from Epsdorff, where he was instructed to liaise with the envoy of the king of Sweden and carry word of political developments in Hanover. To any ambitious courtier this would have been a mission to be savoured. It was a very clear and public sign of the regard in which Ernest Augustus held Königsmarck and once upon a time, Königsmarck would have seized the opportunity with both hands. Once upon a time, of course, Königsmarck hadn't been in love with Sophia Dorothea. Far from promotion, all that the trip meant now was separation from the women he adored.

At first, Königsmarck accepted his fate because he could do no other and besides, Sophia Dorothea would be with her husband in Epsdorff. Better to go to Hamburg, carry out the mission, then come home to Hanover to await her return. All of that stoicism changed when Sophia Dorothea fell suddenly ill and was unable to endure the journey ahead of her. Whilst Königsmarck was in Hamburg and her husband in Epsdorff, Sophia Dorothea would be all alone in Hanover.

The hunting party was due to leave a few days ahead of Königsmarck's departure and he found himself torn, fearing that Sophia Dorothea was seriously ill whilst at the same time hoping that she 'were pretending [to be ill], for love of me' in order to snatch a few days with him before he left for Sweden. Sophia Dorothea's illness was in fact genuine but it wasn't as serious as Königsmarck had feared. The couple resolved to make the best of the unexpected few days they had together but by now George was so distant from his wife that she didn't even know when he was and wasn't in residence. He was supposed to be safely in Epsdorff so imagine Königsmarck's horrified surprise when, whilst making his way to see Sophia Dorothea, he bumped into her husband instead.

'That nuisance of a man turned up so unexpectedly,' wrote the Swede to his paramour, 'I admit I hated him on sight. Thunder from a clear sky could not have surprised me more.' Nor could it have been more inconvenient, and it meant that the lovers had lost their opportunity to spend some uninterrupted time together. When Sophia Dorothea recovered, she was expected to set off immediately to join the hunting party or risk arousing the suspicions of everyone who was already whispering about the count's devotion to her. The Epsdorff party was also planning to visit Göhre and Königsmarck suggested that he and Sophia Dorothea might arrange an assignation there but she refused, sensible enough to realise that the plan was unworkable.

They did, however, manage to snatch an impromptu meeting before Sophia Dorothea's departure and the prevaricating princess put her lover's fevered mind at rest once more. After their meeting, Königsmarck reminded her to take no one into her confidence in the matter of their romance, warning her once more of the power of court gossip and all that they risked. It was advice he would have done well to heed himself.

With Sophia Dorothea gone, Königsmarck decided not to remain in Hanover but instead he left for Hamburg, stopping off along the road to spend some time with his regiment. The letters began again almost immediately and like a lovesick teenager, Sophia Dorothea was the only thing on her lover's mind. Though her replies are lost there's enough in Königsmarck's notes to suggest that she constantly sought reassurance as to his continuing affections and he told her, 'I hope after all these assurances you will not ask me again whether I love you. If you still doubt it will kill me.' It's little wonder that Sophia Dorothea doubted him though, given the loveless marriage which she had been forced to endure. Her husband showed her no affection and denied her even friendship, whilst she had never quite settled in at Hanover. Königsmarck gave Sophia Dorothea the affection she had been starved of and the thought of being without it seems to have been crushing.

There remains that element of absurdity though and nowhere is that more clear than in Königsmarck's decision to take up with a new companion. Let's hear it from the gentleman's own pen; I doubt anyone else could do justice to this particular confession!

> 'I have a consolation here, close to me; not a pretty girl but a bear, which I feed. If you should fail me I will bare my chest and let him tear my heart out. I am teaching him that trick with sheep and calves, and he doesn't manage it badly. If ever I have need of him - God help me! I shall not suffer long.'

No pressure on Sophia Dorothea then, just the constant threat of a massive bear ready to tear Königsmarck's heart out of his chest!

Königsmarck might have a trained bear, but he had reckoned without the influence of Éléonore, Sophia Dorothea's mother. When she received her daughter in Epsdorff, word had already reached her of the gossip that was doing the rounds in Hanover regarding Königsmarck and Sophia Dorothea. She warned her daughter that she was standing on thin ice already and that it was cracking with every step that she took. Sophia Dorothea, always emotional, went into a panic and wrote to her lover to tell him that there was only one thing for it: he must find a wife.

You can imagine how that went down.

'I must marry, since you wish it; it shall be done. I will obey your wishes; it is enough that you will have it so. My death-sentence is inscribed by the hand I adore. I confess I should never have expected to see so dreadful a sentence passed on me by you. But of what am I complaining? I must remember that I have loved you, and I ought to have known the sex better than to believe all you vowed to me. Alas! I was weak and believed it; I must now be firm enough to support the consequences. Your cruelty goes too far, for, unless you wished to wound me, you could never have treated me thus. Why has not God given you a heart less cruel and me a heart less tender? - we should agree better then. I have never been but yours; I wanted to be so all my life, but you do not regard my constancy... You wish me to marry to save myself from destruction, but you do not reflect that marriage would surely bring about my ruin. There are two ways of escape from this dilemma. The first, and the more agreeable to me, is for you not to suffer me to marry; and if my ruin follows, as I foresee, not to forsake me. The second will be easier for you. It is to let me marry; and swear to me on your oath that you will always cherish the affection you have seemed to show me. I will wait until your answer comes, which I hope to receive from your hand (not disguised if you please); and I mean to regulate my conduct accordingly, so that I may have nothing to reproach myself with. But you love me no longer - your head has triumphed over your heart; and it is not even enough that you love me no longer, you wish me to love you no more. What a hard thing! How will it be possible for me to obey? No, Madame, in spite of all, I shall always adore you; my love will be extinguished only with my life. Believe this from your most humble and affectionate servant.'

Sophia Dorothea told her paramour to marry, knowing that such a thing was unlikely to happen because Königsmarck loved the heady excitement that came with his romantic escapades far too much. Yet in all of this beseeching, all of these adolescent outpourings, there is no kindness at all to the woman he purports to love. Like so many of Königsmarck's letters it's page after page of 'poor me', in which Sophia Dorothea is chief among his tormentors, devising ever more cruel ways to make her beloved miserable. The fact that many of her letters to Königsmarck have long since been lost or destroyed is a particularly frustrating fact of life when dealing with these star-crossed lovers but Königsmarck's replies give us plenty of clues as to their content.

And she was more than his match, it seems.

Looking from the distance of centuries, what we appear to have here is a relationship marked by codependency in which two people, each carrying their own emotional baggage and each with a certain degree of emotional immaturity, come together in a perfectly explosive mixture of need and guilt. Sophia Dorothea was a woman who had been babied at home and ignored in marriage. Unlike her mother or her mother-in-law, she had never learned the valuable ways of court politics. When she met Königsmarck, dashing, devoted and a link to that happy childhood in Celle, it was as though someone had lit a match under a firework, but rather than soaring, Sophia Dorothea was flaring and fizzing out again and again and again. With few friends to speak of, let alone to counsel her in how best to handle this rush of emotion, she plunged into a maelstrom that must have left her reeling. She craved the excitement of the affair, the attention of her lover and the human contact that he gave her, not to mention the love she never received from her own husband, but she feared it too. The stakes in this game were enormous and she knew it, so those flares of emotion were followed by a desperate effort to push Königsmarck away.

I love you, go away.

And Königsmarck, handsome, celebrated and desired, was used to getting what he wanted, an alpha male who knew every trick in the book. His fatal fascination with Sophia Dorothea was an intriguing one and it's easy to think that he wanted her precisely because she was married to George, the grumpy, bad-tempered heir, but if all he sought was seduction, then he achieved that time and again. If that was Königsmarck's aim, he would have happily marched off back to his regiment or another conquest's bed. In fact, he found the wild adoration and overheated melodrama of his affair with Sophia Dorothea utterly intoxicating, as though it gave him life in the rigidly disciplined court of Hanover. He enjoyed the game, I think, relishing the embraces that were inevitably followed by a panicked rejection by his mistress and after that, the reconciliation.

Together they played the same game of chess over and over again, each move repeating itself in a loop of love, rejection, recrimination and reunion. In his angry replies to Sophia Dorothea's pleas that he should leave her or marry another, Königsmarck betrayed his own immaturity. Even when acknowledging the danger the couple faced, still he accused her of playing with his affections for her own entertainment. In fact Sophia Dorothea was playing a very dangerous game each time she and Königsmarck went to bed for if another child were to be born, the court gossips would be ready to point the finger. George, though he might be happily ensconced with his own mistress and eventually their three illegitimate children, would never let such a grievous wrong pass.

At times, the decisions the clandestine couple made seem almost absurd. Were their story fictional we might wonder what their author was thinking but they weren't make believe, they were entirely real and their bad decisions and overheated letters were the signs not of an over imaginative creator, but of a couple whose emotional development appears to have stopped somewhere around the age of 15. It was a heady and intoxicating mix.

Whilst he was in Hamburg on the orders of Ernest Augustus, Königsmarck was entrusted with securing an alliance between Hanover and Sweden. It wasn't to be, but Königsmarck so impressed the Swedish king, Charles XI, that the monarch offered him a position in his homeland. It wasn't the first time such an offer had been made and as ever, Königsmarck politely rejected his sovereign's overtures. It seems that for all the drama in his love life, Königsmarck was as impressive a diplomat as he was a soldier and he was certainly respected in both Hanover and Sweden. He had no wish to permanently return to the land of his birth and nor did he need to because whilst he was off adventuring, he left his estates safely in the care of his mother, Maria[14].

Königsmarck had always been a caring son and when he received word of his mother's death during his sojourn in Hamburg, he was heartbroken. She had been a constant in an adventurous, tumultuous life, an anchor to the land of his birth and the one person who had always adored Königsmarck without question. That anchor had now been snatched away and Königsmarck was left reeling. As soon as he had concluded his Hanoverian business in Hamburg the grieving soldier set off for Epsdorff, where he found Sophia Dorothea waiting to receive him with sympathy.

The on again, off again couple were on. Again.

Yet the petulance of Count von Königsmarck was never far away and it burst to the surface when George was struck down with a serious attack of the measles. Hearing that Sophia Dorothea had nursed her ailing husband throughout his sickness, Königsmarck was seized by jealousy. That unattractive selfishness that marked so many of his letters came to the fore as he exclaimed, 'with what grief I hear that you have been in other arms than mine!' The only crumb of comfort he could take from the situation was the sure knowledge that Sophia Dorothea would have been acting under sufferance rather than out of genuine affection for her grumpy husband, who one can't imagine would make a particularly likeable patient.

If Königsmarck hoped that Sophia Dorothea was caring for George through gritted teeth, imagine how annoyed he must have been to realise that wasn't the case at all. In fact, being in such close quarters with her debilitated husband hadn't widened the gulf between the spouses, it had narrowed it. Sophia Dorothea and George emerged from the sickroom as better friends than they had been in years and as she warmed to George, Sophia Dorothea became colder towards Königsmarck. She laid the blame for this change at his door, claiming he had behaved with indifference to her, an accusation that can only raise a smile given the endless stream of adoring, impassioned letters that Königsmarck sent to his lover. If that's indifference, it is mind boggling to imagine what she would have judged attentive!

Faced with her dismissive reaction, Königsmarck told Sophia Dorothea that he was in terminal decline and sobbed that everyone at court believed he was ill. He was so haggard and unhappy that he concocted a lie in which he claimed that he had fallen downstairs and was still recuperating from his injuries. Better they think that, he sniffed, than 'suspect that the true cause of my illness arises from your injustice and disdainful airs.'

In Königsmarck's head George's sickbed was the hottest place on earth and rather than suffering with his measles, the cunning husband was romping with his wife. As anyone who has had measles can attest, romping is the last thing on the patient's fevered mind!

But no mind was more fevered than the jealous Königsmarck.

As George regained his strength Königsmarck sought constant reassurances from his lover, but she wouldn't give them. Worse still, even once her husband was recovered she didn't come home to Hanover but instead went to visit her parents in Celle. Here an anxious Éléonore sought her daughter's assurance that the intrigue with Königsmarck was over and that he would soon be married to another, an act that would put a necessary distance between the count and Sophia Dorothea.

Such assurances were hard to come by and when Königsmarck turned up in Celle, the concerned duchess had her answer. Whether she knew her daughter was already sexually intimate with Königsmarck remains a mystery but it was enough that there was suspicion, and the gossips were whispering more keenly with every passing day. After all, even if Sophia Dorothea was doing nothing more than indulging in a little bit of harmless flirtation, which is what Éléonore dearly wished to believe, innocence would be no barrier to those who might scheme to come between Sophia Dorothea and George. He had already proven that he had a hot temper and all that Sophia Dorothea had was her honour. Should her reputation be sullied, who knows what action George might take in vengeance?

In the comfort of Celle, surrounded by the memories of her happy childhood and with her cool-headed mother there to offer guidance, Sophia Dorothea resolved to end the affair once and for all. She told Königsmarck that he must leave and in reply he wrote a letter that was as cruel as it was overwrought. As you may recall, George's brother, Charles Philip, had been killed fighting in the Morea, a conflict in which Hanover lost thousands of men. The shadow of the war still hung over the land and it was a loss from which Duchess Sophia had barely recovered. Now Königsmarck invoked mention of that battle, stirring up all the unhappiness that went with it and awakening the ghosts of those who had died there. Perhaps, he suggested, it was time for him to join them.

> 'I have had a letter from a friend who is in the same state as myself,[15]- that is why he is going to the Morea. If fortune does not change, I shall go on that expedition with him, and, I hope, never return. Perchance you may be kind enough to have a memorial erected for me; if so, do not forget to inscribe on it that I welcomed death with joy, because I was forbidden to look into your beautiful eyes. Ah, Madame! how you make me suffer! Are these the delights of love?'

This was a peculiarly cruel jab from Königsmarck, who knew that nobody who lived at the Hanover court could fail to remember the tragedy of the young man's death, not to mention those troops who had lost their lives. He calculated precisely how Sophia Dorothea would react and of course she didn't disappoint. She remembered too well the loss of her brother-in-law and Königsmarck's own departure for battle that same year and the thought of him facing such danger again chilled her to the marrow. She begged him to stay where it was safe and he magnanimously said that he would, writing with a sweetness that's likely to rot your teeth, 'I should not go away except on your account, and since you ask me to stay I will do so with joy.'

And a few rather less honourable emotions, no doubt.

Duchess Éléonore might have believed that her little girl was pure as the driven snow and had become the subject of malicious rumours for nothing more serious than a little flirting, but things had progressed far beyond the occasional knowing smile and stolen glance. Sophia Dorothea and Königsmarck's love was flourishing, and there was nothing courtly about it. Sitting in the castle at Celle, under the very nose of his lover's family, he wrote again.

> 'I shall embrace to-night the loveliest of women. I shall kiss her charming mouth. I shall worship her eyes, those eyes that enslave me. I shall hear from her very lips that she loves me. I shall have the joy of embracing her knees; my tears will chase down her incomparable cheeks. I shall hold in my

arms the most beautiful body in the world. Verily, Madame,
I shall die of joy. But so long as I have time to tell thee that
I die thy slave, I care for naught besides.'

Safe to say, knees weren't all that were about to be embraced, and when
Königsmarck wrote of their night together, 'God what a night I have
spent! It makes me forget all my worries, I am the happiest man on
earth,' love was most definitely in the air.

Enter the Duchess

Sophia Dorothea was still at Celle when a strange kerfuffle erupted in
Hanover thanks to the discovery of a supposed conspiracy against Ernest
Augustus, apparently in revenge for his adoption of primogeniture. This
had already been the cause of domestic disharmony when Frederick
Augustus, Sophia and Ernest Augustus' second son, rebelled against
his father's wishes, citing all that he would lose if his elder brother,
George, was to become the sole heir. Ernest Augustus saw nothing to
be so upset about and promised his other sons that they would receive
generous payments as well as every opportunity to make the best of their
futures, but Frederick Augustus refused to be mollified. As a result, he
was thrown out of the house. He turned his back on Hanover in favour of
a military career which ended with his death at the Battle of St Georgen
in Transylvania at the end of 1690, another conflict in the seemingly
endless Nine Years' War.

If Ernest Augustus hoped that the death of his estranged son would
also mark the end of familial opposition to primogeniture, he was to
be sadly mistaken. Now the third son, Maximilian William, came
forward to make his own case against his father. Whilst Frederick
Augustus lived Maximilian William had very little to lose as third
son, but once his brother was dead he saw all that George would
now inherit upon their father's death, and he was bitterly envious.
When his diplomatic efforts to change Ernest Augustus' mind failed,
Maximilian William chose a different route and the fallout shook
Hanover to its foundations.

It all began in December 1691 when two trusted friends of Maximilian
William visited Hanover and brought with them a gift of snuff for Ernest

Sophia Dorothea
of Celle.

Count Philip Christoph
von Königsmarck.

Countess Clara von Platen.

Count Philip Christoph von Königsmarck.

The murder of Count von Königsmarck.

Éléonore Desmier d'Olbreuse, Duchess of Celle.

Electress Sophia. Petrus
Schenck.

Ernest Augustus,
Elector of Hanover.

Sophia Dorothea
of Celle.

Countess Aurora
Königsmarck.

Georgius D.G. Mag. Britanniæ Francia et Hiberniæ Rex. Fidei Defensor

Brun: et Lunen: Dux S.R.I. Arch: Thesau: et Princeps Elector &c. Jnauguratus xx die Octobris 1714

Georgius D.G. Mag. Britanniae Franciae et Hiberniae Rex. John Benson Lossing.

Sophia Dorothea,
Queen in Prussia.
After Johann
Hirschmann.

Ernest Augustus,
Elector of Hanover.

Count Philip Christoph
von Königsmarck.

George Augustus Prince
of Wales, later George II.
Godfrey Kneller. 1724.

Georgius [mus] D. G. Mag: Brit: Fran: et Hib: Rex: F.D.

Brun: et Lunen: Dux: S.R.I. Arch: Thesau: et Princeps Elector &c.

Inauguratus 20 die Octobris 1714.

King George I. John Faber, after D Stevens. 1722.

George William, Duke
of Brunswick-Lüneberg.
Hendrik Causé.

Sophia von Kielmansegg,
Countess of Darlington.
After Godfrey Kneller.

Sophia Dorothea.

Queen Anne. John
Closterman, after John
Faber. 1730.

Sophie Electrice d'Hanouer, Duchesse de Brunsuic, Et Lunebourg, Neé Princeße Electoral Palatine.

Right: Sophia Electress of Hanover, mother of King George I. RB Peake. 1690.

Below: The Castle of Herrenhausen.

De begrafenis van George Lodewyk Koning van Groot Britt: tot Hanover, zynde het doode Lig haam van Osnabrug met grote statie daar na toe gebragt. Op den 6 Sept: 1727. Pet Schenk exc: Amst: cum Pr:

Exsequiæ Georgii Ludovici, Magnæ Britt: Regis Funere ejus e Diæcesi, vulgo dicta, Osnabrug Hanoviam ad ducto, die 6 Sept: 1727.

The Funeral of George I, King of England. Leonard Schenk, after Adolf van der Laan. 1727-1729.

Ahlden House.

Sophia Dorothea's wing at
Ahlden House.

The Coronation of
George I.

Above: Celle Castle.

Right: Horace Walpole. Henry Hoppner Meyer, after Sir Thomas Lawrence. 1795.

Augustus. The duke, suspecting there was nothing more than generosity behind their gesture, offered the snuff to his pet spaniel. The poor pooch died there on the spot.

'The gates have been shut for two days at Hanover, accompanied with a great consternation,' wrote Colt of the events. 'Prince Max [is] secured under guard in his chamber, none of his servants being suffered to come near him; but the Duchess, who is under great affliction, and the Duke, say'd publicly that there were designs against his person and Government, and many storeys are dispersed about.'[16]

Weren't they always?

Chief amongst the rumours was the claim that the omnipresent Anthony Ulrich had a role in the conspiracy, fearing the increase in power that primogeniture would bring to Hanover. After all, with just one man controlling the duchy rather than it being split between brothers as was currently the case, it would become more than a match for his own realm of Brunswick-Wolfenbüttel. Even Duchess Sophia found herself under suspicion, suspected of funding the plot against her husband in order to benefit her son.

All Sophia was really guilty of was being an indulgent mother but that indulgence and love of her boys was echoed by the populace of Hanover, who were far fonder of the disenfranchised Maximilian William than they were of George, even if his father didn't share their preference. As Sophia Dorothea, accompanied by her children and her mother, was arriving back in Hanover ready for the traditional winter carnival in January 1692, Maximilian William was on his way to Hamelin, where he was to be held as a prisoner until enquiries had been completed. In the event, Maximilian William was released from custody and exiled. In a final slap to his father's face, Maximilian William was offered refuge by good old Anthony Ulrich, who was still blanching from Ernest Augustus' efforts to implicate him in the supposed conspiracy. From Wolfenbüttel, Maximilian William eventually travelled on to Austria, where he settled as a trusted soldier of the Holy Roman Emperor until his death in 1726. Some of his supposed coconspirators weren't so lucky and as he enjoyed his freedom they went to their deaths, sending a clear and stark message about the cost of trifling with Ernest Augustus.

Though some of Sophia Dorothea's more adoring biographers have claimed that Clara attempted to implicate her rival in the conspiracy, she was too busy enjoying the carnival to bother.

Sophia Dorothea had no involvement in politics beyond her occasional but open favouritism for the French, and less still in primogeniture. Besides, Ernest Augustus still nursed a fondness for his daughter-in-law and any efforts to implicate her would have been entirely wasted.

Anyway, Sophia Dorothea had more worrying things to think about, as January 1692 also happened to be the month in which Melusine gave birth to her first child by George. That little girl was the first of three children that he would father with his mistress[17] and Sophia Dorothea knew precisely who the daddy was. Once again, the couple had a furious confrontation and once again, George met his wife's fierce recriminations with violence. She longed for Königsmarck's adoring company but whilst Sophia Dorothea had been dealing with rumours of her husband's illegitimate child, someone else had caught Königsmarck's eye. She was Sophie Charlotte of Württemberg, the glamorous Duchess of Saxe-Eisenach, and she had never been one to refuse a compliment nor to avoid a gallant such as Königsmarck. In fact, she positively encouraged it and her reputation as a pleasure-seeker mirrored Königsmarck's own. Barely 21-years-old, Sophie Charlotte arrived in Hanover with her husband, John George II, Duke of Saxe-Eisenach, ready to party. The ever flirtatious Königsmarck was quick to tell Sophia Dorothea of the duchess' efforts to ensnare him whilst assuring her that she need not fear, for he had eyes only for the crown princess.

In fact, he wailed, he was positively besieged!

> 'Did you really notice how the Duchess of Saxe-Eisenach attacked me? I hope when I have answered her two or three times as curtly as possible, she will clearly understand that I want no intercourse with her.'

The Duchess of Saxe-Eisenach must have briefly seemed like a dream come true for Éléonore and no doubt she hoped that Königsmarck, with his well-publicised love of ladies, would capitulate to the noblewoman. Her warning to Sophia Dorothea of the gossip regarding her behaviour had fallen on deaf ears but should Königsmarck enter into an affair with the duchess, then Sophia Dorothea would see what sort of a man her would-be suitor really was and everybody could rest easy.

For once, Königsmarck resisted. This must have come as something of a blow to Éléonore, who was still fearful of the damage the gossip might do to her daughter's reputation. Though Königsmarck and Sophia Dorothea were necessarily discreet during the winter carnival in Hanover, the Duchess of Celle had finally had enough of Königsmarck's meaningful glances.

Her warnings to Sophia Dorothea having gone unheeded, Éléonore approached Königsmarck in private and the pair had a long and, one imagines, rather awkward conversation. Though his mistress' mother was all smiles and civility, Königsmarck suspected that her motivation was less than pure. It was all an act, he suggested, a facade cultivated to conceal the fact that all the time she was trying to poison Sophia Dorothea against him. Königsmarck beseeched his lover to ignore the gossip and instead think of their future. For the first time, they were dreaming of escape.

In a letter written in March 1692, Königsmarck wrote of Sophia Dorothea's suggestion that, 'you are willing to leave all this pomp and splendour and retire with me to some corner of the world.' This might have been something written in the heat of passion but it was a serious matter. With Sophia Dorothea's father-in-law poised to transform his duchy into an electorate and events in England making it increasingly likely that George might one day reign as king there, talk of abandonment was as good as treason.

Yet Sophia Dorothea was once again on the retreat, piqued by the Duchess of Saxe-Eisenach's interest in her lover. When the court and its various hangers on trekked over to Celle to continue the festivities, Sophia Dorothea continued to treat Königsmarck coolly, probably convinced that his claims to find the young noblewoman thoroughly annoying were a case of protesting too much. She knew that nothing aroused his ire more than being ignored, so she determined to blank him completely, refusing to even catch his gaze when they attended events together.

If Sophia Dorothea's aim was to drive him to distraction, it worked. Königsmarck berated his lover furiously, reminding her of 'the sacrifice I have made for you of the Duchess of Saxe-Eisenach', and begging her to meet with him. At first, it seems that he tried to match her disinterest with disinterest of his own, deliberately avoiding Sophia Dorothea at a dance. Once his temper had cooled though, Königsmarck thought better of what he had done and wrote to Sophia Dorothea apologetically, explaining that he hadn't meant to ignore her, but 'the dancing made me very hot, and, as I was unable to change my linen, I did not like to come near you.' Proof if ever we need it that history could be just as sweaty as it was grand!

And of course she forgave him, with another one of those nights spent in rapturous embraces. The Duchess of Saxe-Eisenach's loss, it seemed, was certainly Sophia Dorothea's gain.

The trip to Celle appears to have been a pivotal moment in the relationship between Königsmarck and Sophia Dorothea and the change it brought about in the count was visible to all. The man who had once been famed for his reputation as an adventurer and lover had resisted the considerable charms of the highly desirable and highly available lady from Saxe-Eisenach and she was as surprised as anybody. As her party departed Celle, the duchess sent her lady-in-waiting to bid farewell to Königsmarck and tell him that the change in his demeanour hadn't gone unnoticed or unremarked. Count von Königsmarck, it seemed, was maturing along with his relationship. Even the desperately overheated notes of yore became just slightly more self-aware as the seeds of escape began to take root.

The brief interlude of peace that had accompanied George's battle with the measles had passed too and when the party from Hanover returned home, Sophia Dorothea dared to stay behind in Celle. She excused herself by claiming that she wished to spend more time with her mother and George didn't argue, but instead left with Melusine without saying goodbye to his wife. She wasn't alone for long and Königsmarck managed to extend his own stay in Celle to snatch a few more days with his mistress. Only when he was called to Hamburg to attend his estates did the couple finally part ways, more tightly bound to one another than ever.

It's here that we begin to see Sophia Dorothea's letters to Königsmarck, though they are few and far between as most of them have long since been lost. Unlike her lover, Sophia Dorothea's French is fluent, but she certainly shares his flamboyant self-expression. Like Königsmarck, she too was convinced that she might die for the want of his company and grew so despondent that it was enough even to arouse the sympathy of George.

She *must* have been unhappy!

> 'I spent the stillness of the night without sleeping, and all the
> day thinking of you, weeping over our separation. Never did

a day seem too long to me; I do not know how I shall ever get reconciled to your absence. La Gouvernante [Eleonore von dem Knesebeck] has just given me your letter; I received it with rapture. Rest assured I will do even more than I have promised, and lose no opportunity of showing you my love. If I could shut myself up while you are away and see no one I would do so gladly, for without you everything is distasteful and wearisome. Nothing can make your absence bearable to me; I am faint with weeping. I hope to prove by my life that no woman has ever loved man as I love you, and no faithfulness will ever equal mine. In spite of every trial and all that may befall, nothing will sever me from you. Of a truth, dear one, my love will only end with my life.

I was so changed and depressed to-day that even the Prince, my husband, pitied me, and said I was ill and that I ought to take care of myself. He is right,- I am ill; but my illness comes only from loving you, and I never wish to be cured. I have not seen any one worth mentioning. I went to visit the Duchess [her mother-in-law, Sophia] for a little while, but returned home as soon as possible to have the joy of talking about you [with Eleonore von dem Knesebeck]. La Gazelle's[18] husband came to wish me good-bye; I saw him in my chamber, and he kissed my hand.

It is now eight o'clock, and I must go and pay my court. How dull I shall seem!- how stupid! I shall withdraw immediately after supper, so that I may have the pleasure of reading your letters again, the only pleasure I have while you are away. Farewell, my worshipped one. Only death will sever me from you; all human powers will never succeed. Remember all your promises, and be as constant as I will be faithful.'

This time, for once, all this talk of death proved to be oddly prescient. During the arduous trip to Hamburg, Königsmarck's carriage broke down just outside Hanover. With no wish to go back, he pressed on and was almost drowned when crossing the Elbe. He managed to escape this particular danger only to discover upon his arrival that the predatory Duchess of Saxe-Eisenach also happened to be visiting. She wasted no time in issuing a dinner invitation to the battered Königsmarck. No sooner had the invitation been received than Königsmarck packed up and left, taking new lodgings with the excuse that urgent business had called him away.

Sophia Dorothea would have been delighted to read of her lover's rejection of the duchess but her joy was to be short-lived. She was in Hanover once more and someone, it seemed, was onto our star-crossed couple. Königsmarck wrote to Sophia Dorothea from Hamburg to inform her urgently that her letters appeared to have been opened and resealed with an unfamiliar seal. Fearful that someone was intercepting their correspondence he told her not to write again and to take care at home. As distant as they were, Sophia Dorothea understandably took fright and withdrew once more. The couple's enemies, it seemed, were gathering.

A Long Silence

For all of Königsmarck's fears, Sophia Dorothea was not without support in Hanover. Whatever her breast-beating early biographers might have claimed, this was not a fairytale. She wasn't a princess locked in a lonely tower just waiting to be rescued by the nearest knight on his dashing white charger, but a young lady who was becoming increasingly isolated in her marital home.

Yet Sophia Dorothea wasn't alone and for now at least, her most influential and valuable supporter in Hanover was without a doubt Ernest Augustus, the man whom few dared to disagree with. He had been charmed by his daughter-in-law from the first and Clara could do little to dissuade him of his attachment despite her best efforts. He was refreshed by the young princess' disinterest in court politics and with her friend Melusine installed in George's bed, Clara knew that she had little to fear from Sophia Dorothea as long as she kept her place.

Ernest Augustus had other things to concern him beyond the business of marriage and his in-laws. He was a man of almost limitless ambitions. His lands could never be extensive enough and he was certain that Brunswick-Lüneburg could become a whole lot more than it was. He had nailed his colours to the mast of the Grand Alliance but with each new report from the battlefield, it seemed that neither France nor the Alliance could clinch the overall advantage. As fast as one side claimed a victory it suffered a defeat and the war dragged on in what appeared to be a mutual and arduous deadlock, both sides suffering and celebrating in turn.

The Grand Alliance always took its time in getting anything done. There were so many egos to satisfy that every single move required delicate discussion, promises and favours. Louis XIV, in stark contrast, was just Louis XIV. His power was absolute and he answered to nobody but himself so whenever the Grand Alliance entered its discussion phase, Louis was able to act whilst his opponents were still talking. In 1692 he proved that he even had time for a bit of show and as the Grand Alliance was agreeing who would send troops to where and what they would get in return, Louis strutted into Mons, the city where he had enjoyed such a triumph just the previous year. Here he held a review of his military might, a blaze of colour and a demonstration of power intended to show his enemies that they had picked on the wrong king. William III was still rallying his allies when Louis left Mons and besieged Namur, a strategically vital city that sat on the main road to the Netherlands. The town fell on 5 June and though the citadel defended itself for several weeks, the French succeeded in capturing it on 30 June.

This victory was important to France not only strategically, but in terms of morale too. In order to split his opponent's defences Louis arranged for a simultaneous naval assault on England, planning to send 12,000 Irish Catholic soldiers over the English Channel with the aim of returning James II to the throne. Instead the French navy faced defeat and the king shelved his plans for an invasion of England. The victory at Namur, therefore, was a much-needed win for Louis and the French, and William III was determined that his counter-assault would be triumphant, if he could just get his alliance to agree with each other long enough for him to make his play.

Once again, Ernest Augustus reminded his comrades of his wish to see Hanover became the ninth electorate of the Holy Roman Empire. To the Protestant courts he made no mention of religion but to the Catholic electors he dropped strong hints that he was considering converting to Catholicism, sure that this would smooth away any remaining doubts. Though George William was the older brother Ernest Augustus had no intention of allowing him to take that honour. *He* was to be the first elector, he wouldn't wait in line behind George William.

With time of the essence, William III agreed to throw his considerable diplomatic weight behind the plan and this time, Ernest Augustus knew, there would be no delay. It was all that was needed to finally tip the balance that would send Hanoverian troops to Flanders. With George at their head, they rode out to face the French. Königsmarck, too distracted by the very presence of Sophia Dorothea to think about battle, delayed in Hanover as long as he dared. The man who had been so celebrated for his military prowess now dodged his duty in the hope of stealing a few more moments with his mistress. Eventually he had no choice but to join the fighting and Sophia Dorothea found herself once more alone at court, as her husband and lover fought on behalf of the Grand Alliance. Concealed in Königsmarck's belongings when he went to war was a small portrait of Sophia Dorothea, a token to light his way without her.

Sophia Dorothea emerges from the pages of her few remaining letters as occasionally just a little bit more mature than her lover. When he spoke of dying for the want of her, he knew he could make such florid predictions without any fears of them coming true but now, with Königsmarck once more returned to the battlefield, the threat of death lingered over him. Whoever had intercepted the letters exchanged by the couple was a mystery and in her isolation, Sophia Dorothea now suspected spies at every corner. She replayed every conversation in her head, seeking out hidden meanings and motives in those who she believed threatened her happiness with Königsmarck. She agonised too over her lover's conduct, wondering why he had not taken advantage of George's absence to visit her before his duty took him from Hanover. Was it, wondered Sophia Dorothea, because he had found another? The thought of Königsmarck being unfaithful made her miserable and she even found herself suspecting her mother-in-law of carrying a torch for him after Duchess Sophia, 'spoke much of your beauty and the regularity of your features.' After all, if the hard to impress Sophia could find Königsmarck beautiful then, 'I fear me others will discover [your] comeliness too. It will cost me many tears.'

In fact, the pining Königsmarck wasn't living the high life Sophia Dorothea imagined, and he instead made efforts to avoid the ribald parties of his fellow soldiers, preferring to spend his time alone with thoughts of the woman he had left behind. He warned Sophia Dorothea that Clara had spies in Hanover and it was they who had prevented him from visiting her before his departure, for he feared that he was being watched. Whoever these spies were Königsmarck didn't say, but it's likely that they were the same people who opened the letters Sophia Dorothea had sent him. And it wasn't only those that wished the couple misfortune who had cottoned on to the romance. Königsmarck related a curious anecdote in which a friend had given him a gentle but pointed warning, reminding the career soldier not to let love get in the way of duty. Königsmarck wrote that his friend, Field-Marshal Heinrich von Podewils[19], said as they were settling for the night, 'My dear friend, may God guard thee, but take this advice from me; do not let thy love ever hinder thee from thinking of thy fortune.'

It's at precisely this moment that we might wonder at Königsmarck all over again. He already suspected that Sophia Dorothea's letters had been intercepted by spies of the Platens who were dogging his footsteps and now a trusted friend had intimated that his affair was making him careless and neglectful of his duty. If ever there was a moment to be cautious this was it. If one man had already noticed he was letting his heart rule his head, then we can be sure that others had too. What of George though, riding off to Flanders even as Königsmarck found every excuse to remain in Hanover? What of Clara and her wily spouse, watching all that was unfolding and filing it away for future reference? All of these thoughts must have occurred to Königsmarck as he mused on the latest developments in his love life but still he didn't draw back or warn Sophia Dorothea to be on her guard. Instead, the couple went full steam ahead.

As events would later prove, Königsmarck was right to be suspicious.

With little to detain her in Hanover Sophia Dorothea set out for Brockhausen, one of her father's many country homes, to spend some time with her parents. Here she remained for several weeks, agonised by the fate of her lover as he went into battle. Nothing brought this more sharply into focus than the death of one of her courtier's brothers, known in Hanover as a young and vibrant man. The fate of this unnamed victim of the war threw her into new panic and she waited for word from her lover, convinced that some evil omen attended them. Yet when the reply came it was once again jealous and suspicious. Königsmarck simply couldn't accept that the far-flung Brockhausen was the cause of any delays in the letters that flew back and forth.

Worse still came when Königsmarck learned that Sophia Dorothea had shone at a party given for foreign envoys. He had expected her to be locked away and pining for him but seemed unable to grasp the fact that she simply couldn't indulge in such displays without arousing suspicion. If she did withdraw and refuse to attend gatherings, nobody would believe it was because she was missing George. Instead they would look for another reason and there was already gossip about Königsmarck's interest in her. Besides, we must ask precisely why he equated love with misery. Königsmarck was never really happy unless he believed that Sophia Dorothea was wailing for the want of him. Any suggestion that she was simply going about her day, missing him quietly and constantly, led him to suspect her of all sorts of foul play. When the wife of an officer commented that she had heard he had been supplanted in the heart of an unnamed woman, he was convinced that Sophia Dorothea had betrayed him and angrily pressed the officer's wife for more information, which she coquettishly refused to give. Again we see the immaturity of Königsmarck's nature, the belief that nothing was true unless it was at the extremes of emotion. 'God will punish you,' he told Sophia Dorothea peevishly when he heard that she had dared to smile and attend a party, 'Take heed therefore and beware.'

This time he had gone too far. Though we might wonder why her next letter wasn't one giving Königsmarck his marching orders, Sophia Dorothea asked in her very polite manner just what exactly his problem was. Perhaps, she suggested, what Königsmarck really wanted wasn't her love and devotion, but an excuse to break off the affair. She was tired of his veiled references to other men and infidelity and threw her hands up, declaring that her love was as true as ever even if nothing she could say would convince him. She even suggested that perhaps someone was intercepting their letters precisely to cause them to argue and if that were the case, they had succeeded admirably.

Days passed in which Sophia Dorothea wrote again and again, protesting her innocence and begging for a kind word from Königsmarck. When he finally replied it was to reproach her for attending the gathering of the foreign envoys. She defended herself, even going so far as to speculate on whether Clara had indeed been the one to intercept their letters. She knew too well of Clara's fearsome reputation and wrote, 'If Countess Platen begins to meddle you may imagine what there is to dread', but Königsmarck, too busy being wounded by his own groundless suspicions, gave no reply. The fact that this letter survives suggests that Clara hadn't been the only one intercepting the letters for the sake of mischief at all, as she surely wouldn't have allowed one that named her as a possible adversary to reach Königsmarck. More likely it was simply the delay caused by Königsmarck's march toward the battlefield which meant that his correspondence was always a few days behind. He had never been a patient man, so any delay caused him to suspect that he had been slighted, wronged and forgotten.

Still Sophia Dorothea, watched by her mother and relying on her trusty confidante Knesebeck to act as a go-between, continued to write. Her letters were at first unhappy, but their miserable tone eventually became defensive and finally it seemed as though Königsmarck had pushed his understanding lover too far. She supplied him with a blow-by-blow account of everything that had occurred during the visit of the envoys, as carefully thought out and catalogued as though it was a witness statement expected to stand up in court. Though her tone was rather clipped at first, by the end of the letter Sophia Dorothea was once again telling her lover that she would lay down her life for him, begging him for a word of kindness to end their dispute.

Yet no word came.

Once again Sophia Dorothea fired off letter after letter, almost being caught more than once by her suspicious mother. On several occasions it was only her quick thinking that saved her, as she hid the half-written notes under her bedclothes when they said their goodnights. Eventually, when Éléonore's constant unscheduled appearances in her daughter's room left Sophia Dorothea fearing to take up her pen, Eleonore von dem Knesebeck wrote on Sophia's behalf, seeking some explanation from Königsmarck for his conduct. The letter did the trick and after weeks of silence, Königsmarck replied. He had received five letters from Sophia Dorothea at once, he admitted, and wondered if others might have been similarly delayed or perhaps even lost. Now he was filled with fresh love and apologies gushed from the nib of his pen as he begged his lover to forgive him his silence.

Of course Sophia Dorothea forgave him. She even apologised and as the count prepared to go to war and fight in the bloody battle of Steenkerque, she reminded him that she was his and his alone.

Into Battle

Sophia Dorothea first heard of the counter-attack on Namur from her husband. When she received his letter, her first thought was of the danger her lover would face as he joined the forces attempting to breach French defences at Steenkerque. William's forces attacked as day dawned on 24 July 1692, catching the French off guard and scoring a surprise assault that ensured the soldiers of the Grand Alliance dominated the early stages of the battle. But George had reckoned without General Luxembourg[20], the man at the head of the French contingent who had been personally entrusted with the protection of Namur by Louis XIV.

Though they initially had the upper hand, the troops of the Grand Alliance, under the command of Ferdinand Willem, Duke of Württemberg-Neuenstadt[21], failed to press their advantage. At the command of Hendrik Trajectinus, Count Solms[22], the mounted cavalry struggled over difficult terrain and caused a blockage that held up the infantry advance. Luxembourg used the time he had wisely, regrouping his soldiers and preparing to throw everything they had into the defence of Steenkerque. Eventually, with the Grand Alliance soldiers in disarray and confusion, William III ordered a retreat. When the smoke cleared both sides had lost more than half their soldiers and the blame was placed on the shoulders of Count Solms, the man whose cavalry had caused confusion and disorder amongst the foot soldiers.

Five British regiments were decimated. The outcry in England was huge and the public called for assurances that in the future, only English generals would be allowed to command English troops. The victory might have been decisive for Louis XIV if only his planned naval assault on England hadn't been foiled by his foe. But for that fortunate turn of nautical events, William III would have been in the direst straights imaginable.

The forces of the Grand Alliance lost more than 8,000 men at Steenkerque, but by some miracle Königsmarck wasn't among them. George hadn't been at the battle as his regiments had been held in reserve and weren't called to fight. In fact, Königsmarck too had been placed in reserve. Rediscovering something of the military fire that had made his name he volunteered, receiving special permission from George to go into battle with another regiment. He took just one of Sophia Dorothea's letters with him onto the battlefield. The others were placed with her portrait in a sealed package and given to a trusted officer with instructions to burn the parcel should Königsmarck be killed. This time he had not let love stand in the way of duty.

With news trickling in of the ferocity of the engagement, Sophia Dorothea's thoughts were all for her lover. Her days passed in agony as she waited for news from the front and with reports coming in of fighting so fierce that the opposing forces of France and the Grand Alliance were literally toe-to-toe on the battlefield, her imagination ran wild. She no longer slept and each day without word made her suffering that much more acute.

'I hate King William, who is the cause of it all,' Sophia Dorothea wrote in a letter to Königsmarck, little knowing when or even if he would ever see it. 'He breaks my heart by thus risking all I have in the world.' She must have been ecstatic to receive a letter from Königsmarck dated after the battle, bringing with it the sure proof that he had survived even that fierce engagement. Though Sophia Dorothea's father had lost a vast number of his men at Steenkerque, this was a mere footnote for her. She cared only for the count.

Sophia Dorothea, who had been like a ghost at court, now came back to life and everyone around her noticed. To her amusement they assumed that her happiness was the result of George remaining safe but she didn't think about her husband, she admitted, only of Königsmarck. With the knowledge that she had come close to losing him never far from her mind, Sophia Dorothea began to plot more and more seriously about how she might make a future with the man she loved. Even the dramatic writings of Königsmarck seemed tempered by the fact that he now had more than intrigue and romance to fill his days and it was with excitement that he told Sophia Dorothea that he had already been invited to the next carnival at Hanover. He warned her that she would hardly know him, burnished by the sun and with a dozen grey hairs in his celebrated curls. Worst of all, that stunning waist-length barnet had been nothing but a hindrance on the muddy battlefields of Flanders and Königsmarck had been forced to take the scissors to his crowning glory. To Sophia Dorothea, none of that mattered. Count von Königsmarck would soon be home again.

It was just the tonic Sophia Dorothea needed as she set out for a visit to Wiesbaden with her mother. Here she was due to spend six stultifying weeks, but the stay was brightened by the arrival of a gift from

Königsmarck of his portrait. With a lull in fighting, Königsmarck's letters regaled Sophia Dorothea with scandalous gossip of his fellow soldiers, whilst promising that he remained true and reminding her to be likewise. When she informed him that she would be leaving Wiesbaden early to take a trip to the Frankfurt fair, his suspicions went into overdrive but she soothed his troubled soul, assuring him that the planned trip was her mother's idea. There was always a hint of the coquette about Sophia Dorothea at moments like this though because as quickly as she assured Königsmarck that he need not worry, she mentioned that an unnamed Prince of Hesse had requested an audience with her, one that was clearly intended to be amorous. Of course she would resist, and it would be a dull event without Königsmarck there to make it sparkle, she told him sweetly.

In fact, in her delight at Königsmarck's survival and her excitement at his imminent return to Hanover, Sophia Dorothea had neglected to observe the age old proverb that she should keep her friends close and her enemies closer. When Clara saw the change in Sophia Dorothea's demeanour from distracted misery as the men went to war to unrestrained delight when she learned of Königsmarck's safety, that raw nerve of hers was once again tweaked into life. What infuriated Clara even more was the fact that Ernest Augustus, the man who shared her bed, seemed not to care about his daughter-in-law and her intrigues with the dashing count.

Ernest Augustus was no less fond of Sophia Dorothea than ever and he knew that George wasn't an easy husband or a faithful one, so the thought of his wife indulging in a few harmless flirtations didn't worry him unduly. At a time when Hanover needed all the able men it could get, Königsmarck was one of its shining military stars and he was respected across the continent. As far as Ernest Augustus was concerned, this was a boat that didn't need rocking.

But Clara was never a woman who liked the word *no*.

The Scheming Mistress

How and why Clara's suspicions were freshly stirred up we can't know for sure but with so many letters flying back and forth, the possibility that some fell into her hands isn't one we should easily discount. The circumstantial evidence of Sophia Dorothea's changing demeanour would have been suspicious in itself and Clara was determined to push a wedge between the lovers. Whilst much of her motivation was plain jealousy there was another matter to consider too, that of Ernest Augustus' age. He wasn't getting any younger nor was he getting any healthier and with Hanover poised on the verge of becoming an electorate, George would one day inherit all that his father and uncle controlled. Clara, cunning and always able to take a long view, saw clearly that it was in her best interests to stay on the right side of the heir. If she could do that by preventing the embarrassment that would be caused should Sophia Dorothea and Königsmarck elope together, then so much the better. The third and final motive behind her actions was the simple matter that Clara absolutely loved drama and there was nothing she liked more than to light the touch paper then sit on the sidelines watching the fireworks - her ploy with the embroidered glove more than proves that!

Frederick, Elector of Brandenburg, and the husband of Ernest Augustus' daughter, Sophia Charlotte[23], had found himself in his father-in-law's sights as Ernest Augustus continued to gather support for his claim to make Hanover an electorate. As a result, Sophia Charlotte, known as *Figuelotte*, and Sophia Dorothea began to spend time in each other's company during official visits. It was during one of these visits that Figuelotte mentioned that Aurora von Königsmarck, who had been such an important go-between in the exchange of letters when the lovers were in Hanover, was to be banished on the say-so of Clara.

The countess, on finding that her lover had little interest in censuring Sophia Dorothea, had changed tack. She told Ernest Augustus that the rumours about Sophia Dorothea and Königsmarck were as loud and scandalous as ever and that Aurora, who was currently visiting Hamburg, was one of the main reasons that the gossip wouldn't die a death. When the Königsmarck siblings returned to Hanover, Clara cautioned, everyone would once again suspect that Aurora's purpose was to provide a cover for the supposed lovers to meet. The Königsmarcks had decided to take a luxurious house together that would make a perfect love nest for a princess, Clara sniffed, and whether the rumours regarding Königsmarck and Sophia Dorothea were true or not, it was probably better to stop them before they could start. If this was what it took to silence Clara's dire warnings, Ernest Augustus decided that it was a small price to pay. He sent word to Hamburg via Marshal Podewils to inform Aurora that she shouldn't return to Hanover and she, understandably furious at such an insult, was happy to oblige.

Upon hearing that one of her few friends had been banished, Sophia Dorothea's usual composure deserted her. Both she and Königsmarck failed to grasp the true motive behind Clara's actions and thought instead that her venom had been directed at Aurora. Indeed, when Sophia Dorothea heard Count von Platen refer to Aurora as a *she-devil*, she rebuked him and, as she proudly noted, he soon fell silent. Sophia Dorothea was close enough to the centre of the storm to sense it brewing and she feared being separated from her lover more than anything.

'I believe with a little prudence and good behaviour one could remedy all these evils,' Sophia Dorothea wrote and she was right, but prudence was something that the couple never seemed able to show. With precious few friends to call her own Sophia Dorothea took Figuelotte into her confidence and learnt that plans were afoot to send Königsmarck on a distant mission that would keep him from Hanover. The only comfort she could derive from her findings was that as far as Figuelotte knew, Sophia Dorothea's name hadn't been mentioned in connection with the plan to have Königsmarck kept from Hanover.

Königsmarck wasn't so sure and he vowed to take revenge on Clara. In his passion he decided to, 'seek out her son, pick a quarrel with him, and send him to the other world'. Of course, he did no such thing. Instead he continued to pour out his heart to Sophia Dorothea in their letters as she did to him, telling him that she had found a new and trusted confidante in the Electress of Brandenburg.

Königsmarck didn't share his lover's trust of her sister-in-law but when Figuelotte came up with a plan that would ensure he was able to remain at court, he was desperate enough to consider it. If Clara was really motivated by anger because Königsmarck had ended their affair, then would it be too great a price to pay to return to her arms? He could flirt a little, whisper some charming words, bestow a few kisses and just like that, he would find himself welcome in Hanover once more.

The very idea of it must have been sickening for Sophia Dorothea but to keep her lover close by, she was willing to put the suggestion to him. Königsmarck was a little more circumspect and wondered whether Figuelotte had conceived the plan merely to test Sophia Dorothea's reaction to it. Perhaps she hoped the princess would betray herself by dismissing the idea but she didn't, because above all she wanted to keep Königsmarck near, remembering too well how close she had come to losing him on the battlefield.

Königsmarck dismissed the idea of renewing his acquaintance with Clara out of hand but Sophia Dorothea was finally decided. She would make her own peace with the countess and hope that it would be enough. As she went to stay with the electress in Brandenburg Königsmarck was stuck in limbo. Though the Flanders campaign had ended for the winter, his application for leave had not been approved. George went home to Hanover and from there to Celle but Königsmarck was left to drag his heels at the military garrison in Dist, with nothing to entertain him. Even the nuns with whom he was lodged proved uninspiring. 'Not like those of Venice', he informed Sophia Dorothea archly.

Then, just as Königsmarck was lamenting the discovery of a dozen new grey hairs in his once lustrous coiffure, a miracle happened.

> 'Who shall hinder *Leopold*, supported by the Suffrages of all the Electors, from erecting into an Electorate Two potent Dukedoms [Hanover and Celle], which are suddenly to be re-united? [...] Considering the ready Inclinations of the Emperor, the Pope, the Electors and the King of *Sweden*, and some other Princes of the Empire, this Prince [Ernest Augustus] cannot fail of being advanc'd to the Electoral Dignity; They may drill out their Opposition for some time; but the principal Obstructions being remov'd the Business will be effectively accomplish'd in the end.'[24]

After years in the balance, the future of Hanover as an electorate finally looked as though it was on the verge of being secured and with just a few palms left to grease, Ernest Augustus and George left for Celle and an audience with George William. Though Königsmarck couldn't publicly leave Dist for Hanover without official permission on pain of being considered a deserter, he could certainly do so secretly and when Sophia Dorothea wrote and told him to hasten to her side whilst her husband and father-in-law were away, he swung into action.

At the promise of his lover's arms, Königsmarck was tireless. For six days and nights he travelled to join Sophia Dorothea, arriving on 8 November 1692. He hastened immediately to the quarters of George Conrad Hildebrandt, his trusted secretary, where he went into hiding and wrote to Sophia Dorothea to inform her that he was home.

And raring to go.

The couple had been apart for more than six months so it doesn't take too much imagination to surmise how they spent the evening of their reunion. All the brief time they were together Königsmarck thought nothing of the inevitable punishment he would face when at last he declared himself to Podewils. The marshal would certainly have been made aware of his departure from Dist, but the lovesick count didn't care. He sought only the comfort of Sophia Dorothea's embraces and if that meant he would be banished to his Hamburg estates for a suitable period of punishment, then so be it. At least he was unlikely to be cut down by French troops, even if he might die of boredom.

Eventually Königsmarck had to go back to the real world and he presented himself to Podewils unflinchingly, waiting to hear what penalty he would face. Podewils wasn't only an old soldier though, it appeared that he might be an old softy too. Since Königsmarck was in Hanover he might as well stay there, the marshal decided. There was little sense in sending him off to Hamburg only for him to return a few months hence. It was Podewils, you may recall, who had warned his protégé against letting his heart cloud his head and if he ever needed proof that his warning had been ignored, Königsmarck's arrival in Hanover was certainly that. As a fellow Huguenot, Podewils had always been sympathetic to Éléonore's plight when she was forced to leave France and he had known Sophia Dorothea all her life, so he certainly had no wish to enter the whispering campaign against her. His decision might be seen as an act of kindness but surely Königsmarck remembered the warning the marshal had offered on the eve of battle. Podewils had done all he could though, now it was up to the lovers to ensure discretion.

As far as Sophia Dorothea was concerned, only one thing remained to be done. Königsmarck must make his peace with Clara as she had attempted to do herself. With some grumbling, he finally agreed to her request though he promised only to be, 'civil to her, even friendly […] but never could I make her believe I liked her, hating her as I do.' Civil was enough for Sophia Dorothea though, so civil it would be.

Even better, when George and Ernest Augustus returned from Celle it was just a brief stopover before they were off again, this time to Berlin. Sophia Dorothea was expected to accompany her husband but instead, as many schoolchildren have done to shirk double maths, she pretended to be ill. So successful was her charade that even the court physician declared her unfit for travel and recommended that she stay behind for the sake of her health to undergo a course of completely unnecessary treatment. Königsmarck was delighted and told her with barely restrained joy, 'the Duchess told me you were very unwell and the Prince said so too […], mind you do not undeceive them!'

Finally the lovers were able to meet without fear of discovery, believing that any intriguing against them was over. At long last they could indulge themselves in a little bit of fun.

'Last night makes me the happiest and most satisfied man in the world. Your embraces showed me your tenderness and I could not doubt your love,' wrote Königsmarck. For once, if only briefly, all was well in Hanover.

The Ninth Electorate

Dreams were coming true all over Hanover, it seemed, and Ernest Augustus had finally received the news that he had sought for so long. He had hustled, fought, schemed and alienated members of his own family and sacrificed thousands of Hanoverian soldiers in the name of ambition but in December 1692, it all paid off.

Ernest Augustus had kept his half of the deal and committed his troops to the Holy Roman Empire. Now it was Emperor Leopold's turn, but the road to the electorate wasn't an easy one. There were few among the eight existing electors who relished the prospect of having their power further split and the Catholic electors of Bohemia, Bavaria, and Duchess Sophia's ancestral lands of the Palatinate feared that creating another Protestant electorate would tip the balance too far in favour of Protestantism. The Protestant electors of Saxony and Brandenburg, meanwhile, feared increasing the influence of Brunswick at the expense of Wolfenbüttel, where Duke Anthony Ulrich already had precious little love for his neighbours in Hanover.

In the end it was the lobbying of William III and Ernest Augustus' son-in-law, the Elector of Brandenburg, that tipped the balance. In Hanover Count von Platen couldn't sit idly and wait for news, so with the duke's permission he sent Otto Grote, Baron zu Schauen, to Vienna to carry out negotiations on the more delicate stages of the discussions. Grote was a masterly diplomat and eventually, once the egos were smoothed and the deals and counter-deals brokered, the outcome was announced.

Hanover was to be recognised as the ninth electorate of the Holy Roman Empire. Grote sealed the deal in December 1692, when he went down on his knees before Leopold and ceremonially presented him with the oath of allegiance. Though it would be many years before the 'i's were dotted and the 't's' crossed and every opponent was mollified[25], the show could finally start.

And Ernest Augustus was more than ready to bask in the spotlight.

The official investiture of the new elector took place in Vienna and when Ernest Augustus, Elector of Hanover, came home in March 1693, it was to a massive celebration. The entire court gathered in the Leineschloss and at the heart of the gathering sat Ernest Augustus and Sophia, the triumphant Elector and Electress. Ernest Augustus placed the electoral cap upon his own head and declared, 'By the grace of God we assume this earthly dignity', and the deed was done. Hanover was on its way to the top.

Yet there was one person whose smile wasn't quite as wide as everyone else's at the party. Königsmarck might have been spared punishment for absconding from his garrison without leave, but that didn't mean that he wasn't censured just a little. Watching Sophia Dorothea playing happy couples with her husband for the sake of the celebrations, he grew jealous of George all over again. She was an Electoral Princess now, and in his fevered mind he was convinced that someone that grand wouldn't possibly look twice at a soldier, even the soldier to whom she had declared her love and spent many risky if happy nights beneath the covers.

To make matters worse, Königsmarck was finding his finances increasingly stretched by his flamboyant lifestyle in Hanover. Those extravagant parties and showy houses came at a price, not to mention the stables that held more than fifty horses and a household staff that was only marginally smaller than that of Count von Platen, the long-serving chief minister. Even worse, without his late mother's guiding hand, the estates Königsmarck had inherited were not proving quite so easy to manage. She had shielded him from the vast majority of his obligations, making sure that all his outgoings were met and his monies monitored, but now that was up to him. Trying to find someone as trustworthy and savvy as his late mother had been quite the task and Königsmarck's agents proved themselves as bad with money as the man himself. His debts, including some to the King of Sweden himself, grew larger and his creditors became more and more fractious until Königsmarck's agents asked him to come home to Sweden and sort out his affairs.

He didn't, of course.

When 1693 dawned George returned to the front. Königsmarck, facing massive gambling debts in Flanders and unable to tear himself away from Sophia Dorothea, stayed in Hanover. He hoped in vain for a promotion and a pay increase to go with it but received neither, perhaps as a result of Clara's unhelpful intervention or simply due to the rumours of a clandestine romance with Sophia Dorothea that were now swamping the court. Essentially, he was being subtly dismissed, the lack of promotion a clear hint from the elector that he should seek employment elsewhere, somewhere far from Hanover. The thought of leaving Sophia Dorothea was one that Königsmarck refused to countenance so instead he remained. He partied, gambled and lived like a man with money to burn but in reality, he was drowning in debt.

Just when it seemed that things couldn't get any worse, they did. The Swedish king, Charles XI, was one of those who looked darkly on the promotion of Hanover to an electorate and his relations with Ernest Augustus had grown increasingly frosty as a result. He decided that the time had come to tempt Königsmarck, a native Swede, away from Hanover and summoned him home with the offer of a promotion to general and an eye-watering salary to match. On top of that, if Königsmarck didn't settle his debts to the Swedish monarch, then he might find his estates in his homeland seized by the crown. Despite this threat still Königsmarck declined, determined to remain in Hanover with the woman he adored. Yet even as he dug his heels in, Sophia Dorothea was increasingly kept from his company, sent to her family in Celle or for visits to Brandenburg and beyond. During a family visit to Luisberg the elector insisted that his son, Maximilian William, be quartered in the neighbouring rooms to Sophia Dorothea. It was an insult too far.

Once exiled for supposedly conspiring against his father, Maximilian William was welcome at court once more and Ernest Augustus was using him to keep a watchful eye on Sophia Dorothea. She was furious and insisted that he be moved, after which she flatly refused to leave her room until they had left Luisberg. There was no proof that Max had romantic designs on his sister-in-law, but Sophia Dorothea clearly believed that he did. Even when she was in Hanover, Sophia Dorothea was surrounded by watchful ladies who contrived to keep her from spending too much time with Königsmarck.

'[Electress Sophia] praises you so highly that were she younger I should be jealous. I really I think she is fond of you,' wrote the oblivious Sophia Dorothea to Königsmarck, exhibiting a staggering lack of common sense. The Electress of Hanover had no more romantic interest in the Swede than she did in any other dashing rake, but she was a shrewd woman and I think it's rather more likely that she was sounding out her daughter-in-law's own opinion on the count, hoping to seek some insight into the rumoured relationship. Sophia Dorothea, however, assumed that everyone was after her lover and told him that, '[Sophia] can hardly show [her appreciation of Königsmarck] more and it makes me quite uncomfortable.'

Rather than realise the danger of discovery the couple contrived to meet during a trip to Brockhausen, and as the Electoral Prince fought in Flanders, his wife and her lover were briefly together once more. At the same time, Königsmarck found himself under siege from Clara and though he did all he could to excuse himself from her invitations, he was convinced that it was but a matter of time before she deduced exactly why his good spirits had deserted him. To Sophia Dorothea's dismay, Königsmarck capitulated and visited Clara's home for supper, where he barely spoke a word and left as soon as he dare. Once again jealousy reared its head, with Maximilian William the imagined threat on one side and Clara on the other, but Sophia Dorothea warned Königsmarck that he must continue to pay court to Countess von Platen, if only to keep her from making the mischief that she so enjoyed.

Another threat was coming from Scandinavia, where Sweden and Denmark had finally tired of the unwieldy Grand Alliance. Sabres were rattling against Hanover and George William in particular, whose heavily fortified territory of Ratzeburg neighboured Holstein, which was in Danish hands. The Danes demanded that he demolish the fortifications, citing them as a threat to Denmark, but George William and Ernest Augustus refused, going against the wishes of the Holy Roman Emperor, who hoped to keep the peace against the odds. Growing ever wearier of his enforced separation from Sophia Dorothea, Königsmarck once again volunteered to fight should he be required to do so. It was a canny move, because it meant that he appeared to be dutifully supporting Hanover even as it also meant that he must stay in the duchy in case he was needed to face a threat from Holstein.

Podewils renewed his warnings of the need for discretion and this time, he told Königsmarck that the rumours did indeed originate with Clara. The only scant comfort in all of this was his assurance that Ernest Augustus had no serious suspicions about the couple, which was a relief to both.

The lovers were fast hurtling towards only one conclusion: that they simply couldn't bear to live apart from one another. Sophia Dorothea went to her father and asked him if she could be given an allowance and an establishment of her own. In itself this wasn't unusual, because she inhabited a world in which showing off was just the done thing. Everyone was engaged in a game of one-upmanship but until that point, when the rumours about Königsmarck reached their loudest, Sophia Dorothea had been ambivalent about joining in with the crowd. Her request for money ran the risk of raising suspicions about her motives but either way, with the threat of a war with Denmark and Sweden on the horizon, George William simply didn't have cash to spare. Instead he told her to go home and make the best of the husband she had, rather than harbour dreams of setting herself up in her own establishment. The result of this was an enormous argument between the Duke and Duchess of Celle, the like of which Sophia Dorothea had never seen before. Her parents rarely fell out but this time, the row was volcanic. For the first time, Sophia Dorothea saw how determined her father was that she wouldn't get her way and for the first time, she began to fear that she was as good as on her own.

Instead of taking her father's advice and making the best of a very bad lot, Sophia Dorothea scoured her marriage contract, hoping that she might find a clause that entitled her to some financial aid. She found none but instead realised that George, 'is absolutely master of everything, for there is nothing I can dispose of without his consent. Even the clause about my dower is so badly worded that they can easily cheat me and take it away.' Hoping for some comfort, she petitioned her mother for an increase in her allowance that would offer some measure of freedom. Knowing that the situation was likely hopeless, Éléonore offered instead to sell her jewels and to give the profits to her daughter, but first promised to speak to George William again. This time, perhaps feeling guilty about his earlier outburst, he was a little more amenable and promised that he would do what he could.

What he could do was far short of what his daughter wanted.

Beset by creditors Königsmarck could offer nothing but words of encouragement and blame, sure that Clara and her old co-conspirator, Bernstorff, were behind George William's refusal to meet his daughter's demands. Even after voicing that suspicion he took delight in baiting the countess, publicly refusing to walk her into dinner despite Sophia Dorothea's reluctant reminder that they should do all they could to keep Clara sweet, even if she couldn't resist a few barbs of her own. She wrote that, 'the Electress told my mother that nothing could be more hideous than La Platen's yellow cloak. I rejoice that neither she nor her cloak will come in my way.'

How wrong events would prove her.

That summer Königsmarck was sent off to face the Danes. He was in Sophia Dorothea's arms when his marching orders arrived and returned home to find that his company was waiting for him. He had no choice but to leave immediately for Celle, the first stop on the road to the battlefield. After a short period as a guest of Sophia Dorothea's mother and father he arrived at the front on the banks of the Elbe, whilst at her marital home, his lover waited anxiously for events to unfold.

Perhaps sensing Sophia Dorothea's vulnerability, Clara sweetly became her rival's most enthusiastic defender. She alone understood that Sophia Dorothea's absence on the court social scene was caused not by intrigue but by her naturally retiring nature. The woman who had schemed against the lovers at every turn suddenly had a change of heart, or so she wanted them to believe, and told Sophia Dorothea that the gossip about Königsmarck hadn't come from her at all, but from none other than Electress Sophia. And Sophia Dorothea, with few friends to call her own, was entirely taken in. After a three hour heart to heart with the countess, Königsmarck's lover told him, 'At last [Clara and I] parted as intimates; no friendship could have been confirmed by more promises than she made me.'

Again we must marvel at her inability to see what was in front of her. Clara's gossipy nature was well known but after months of suspicion and doubt about her, all it took for Sophia Dorothea to change her opinion was one girly chat.

For once, Königsmarck was a little less credulous than the electoral princess. He warned her not to drop her guard and admitted that he hoped, 'you will be wise enough not to tell her anything that might do you the least harm. [...] You must look upon her as one of your greatest enemies.'

Little did either of them know just *how* great.

A Bad Lot

For all their sabre-rattling over the disputed fortifications at Ratzeburg, when the moment came for Denmark and Sweden to face the dukes and settle the matter by force, Sweden lost its taste for the fight. There seemed little appetite for blood on either side and the outbreaks of hostilities were punctuated by periods of truce and negotiation but for Königsmarck at the front, the risk was real. George was once again in Flanders and Sophia Dorothea, staying with her parents in Celle, couldn't fail to have been aware of the threat to her homeland. If the Danes were able to pacify Ratzeburg then Celle and Hanover were the next obvious territories for assault.

It seemed as though everyone was falling ill too, with an outbreak of dysentery and fever causing Podewils, Königsmarck, and many other men to take to their beds. Sophia Dorothea was likewise taken ill and languished for some time. She lost weight and, she worried, her lustre, but Königsmarck assured her that she needn't fret, because it was her soul that he adored. George was already home from Flanders and it had been suggested that he might like to at least attempt to show his wife some attention, were the rumours regarding her to be quashed. George wasn't exactly keen but nor was he particularly resistant, so the overture was made and Sophia Dorothea was summoned home. There was nowhere she would rather less be than in Hanover but with Celle sitting in the path of a possible Danish advance, nor could she reasonably argue that she would be safer in her homeland. Likewise, Sophia Dorothea's illness had passed and with it, the last excuse for staying away from Hanover. Reluctantly she was forced to join her husband. She did so in body only. Her heart was far away.

Königsmarck wasn't immune from attempts to interest him in other ladies either. Whilst he was encamped, Count Niels Bielke[26] suggested that his own daughter might make an admirable bride for the soldier. Königsmarck refused so vociferously that the count couldn't help but be offended, especially when the perspective groom declared that he would rather starve in the gutter than marry the lady!

The count's thoughts were all for Sophia Dorothea. Though her letters to him during this period didn't survive, it seems that she rather overdid the ignoring George bit. In fact, Königsmarck even counselled her to show her husband at least a little warmth, if only to head off any suspicions that might arise were she rude to him. Whether it was politically or personally, it seemed that 1693 was a year of bad tidings in Hanover. Though the Danes claimed the upper hand in the conflict and Königsmarck was finally allowed to return to Hanover, he could see little of his lover nor could she see much of him.

In George's bed once more, Sophia Dorothea's guilt at her clandestine romance appears to have taken her by surprise. She began to believe that her illness and the tribulations of her family - her father faced possible ruin should Denmark advance on Celle - were a punishment from God for the sins that she had committed against her marriage vows. The liaisons between the couple were short and infrequent and when they were in society together, Sophia Dorothea pointedly ignored Königsmarck. Even worse was when she missed their appointed meetings altogether, leaving him standing outside in the freezing darkness waiting for an embrace that never came.

When she was in Celle, Sophia Dorothea had allowed herself to dream that this might be the start of her longed-for escape. Her father's lack of ready cash had put paid to that so now, in Hanover, she did as she was told. She returned to the company of her husband, smiled in public and did nothing that might give away her feelings for Königsmarck, but life must have been miserable. George hadn't given up his mistress and all of this happy family show was just that, a performance. It won't come as a surprise to learn that nobody was more taken in by it than Königsmarck and he beat his breast that she would appear happy without him, neglecting to acknowledge not only that he had warned her to show her husband some warmth, but also the inescapable fact that Sophia Dorothea couldn't risk arousing the suspicion of those around her.

Just as the letters the lovers exchanged had apparently been intercepted before, now it seemed that someone in Hanover was helping themselves to the couple's correspondence again. Königsmarck urgently warned Sophia Dorothea to ensure that none of her stash had been misplaced. He also begged her to ensure that Knesebeck knew the official line were she questioned. The lady-in-waiting must say that any letters were for her and her alone. Königsmarck intended to make sure that his own go-betweens would pretend no knowledge of the identity of the woman concerned other than the pseudonym, *Frole Crunbuglen*. Beyond that, each must deny ever having written to the other at all.

Königsmarck now gave up all hope of further advancement in the Hanoverian army. With Sophia Dorothea's pleas for her own establishment falling on deaf ears, the only thing left was for her lover to find some way to settle his debts then, as soon as possible, for the couple to flee Hanover.

Until fate stepped in the shape of Clara, bringing with her the repeat of an earlier offer.

She could wipe away every worry Königsmarck had, she told him, if in return he would take her daughter, Sophia[27], as his wife. With the marriage would come financial stability, a return to favour in Hanover and a bright future, just a bright future in which Clara was his mother-in-law. This suggestion was one that Königsmarck barely even countenanced. He reminded Clara that there were very good reasons why he couldn't marry her daughter, namely the fact that he and Clara had, once upon a time, been lovers. The thought of it was too much and with his refusal, the last nail was hammered into his coffin.

Clara wasn't just a woman scorned.

She was a woman scorned *twice*.

It's impossible to know whether Königsmarck was ever tempted to accept Clara's offer but I think it's unlikely. He was a man of absurdly fiery passions and one who required precious little prodding to fall into extremes of happiness and misery, so marriage to Clara's offspring would certainly have found him permanently in the latter state. Instead he determined to find other means to solve his problems, but solutions needed money and money was one thing he certainly didn't have.

So where could a soldier go when the cash ran out?

Königsmarck's first port of call was Hamburg, but he found little comfort there. Doors were closing all around and as 1694 dawned, the count's situation was precarious indeed. If that wasn't enough to worry about, Ernest Augustus fell so ill that for a time there were fears for his life and with them, renewed concerns regarding the Königsmarck, Sophia Dorothea affair. If Ernest Augustus was to die, then George and Sophia Dorothea would succeed as Elector and Electress of Hanover and if that were the case, there could be no question of a lover muddying the waters. Without Ernest Augustus, Clara's influence would be significantly reduced and there was every reason to believe that Sophia

Dorothea wouldn't waste any time in putting the scheming countess firmly in her place once she was the one who held the reins.

If Königsmarck and Sophia Dorothea were to escape, it seemed as though it was now or never. It was now or never for Clara too, and as her lover grew sick, a woman as intelligent as she was cannot have failed to have grasped the implications. She wielded an unmatched power at court but that power depended on her association with the elderly elector. George, waiting to take his father's place, had never shared Ernest Augustus' fondness for Clara and when the electoral cap sat on *his* head, all of that power and influence would be lost.

It's easy to see Clara's motives as nothing more than spite, twisting the knife into the woman Königsmarck had abandoned her for because she wrongly thought that Ernest Augustus wasn't long for the world. In reality, Clara was too smart to strike for such a simple reason. If she was going to cause mischief, she needed to get something out of it other than sadistic satisfaction.

So what could Clara gain from disgracing Sophia Dorothea? If her marriage to George went south, what was in it for the countess?

Put simply, it was a continuation of influence. Clara had twice suggested her daughter, Sophia, as a possible bride for Königsmarck but the idea had gone nowhere fast. Sophia was almost certainly George's half-sister by Ernest Augustus and she was one of the crown prince's closest allies and most intimate friends. Through her, Clara could enjoy some influence over her lover's heir but George had never shown any particular fondness for Clara herself. If she were the one to finally provide evidence of his wife's affair with Königsmarck, before George faced the embarrassment of his electress having betrayed him and perhaps even abandoned him, then Clara firmly believed that it would only increase her standing with George. After all, should Sophia Dorothea ditch George once he had succeeded as elector, the embarrassment would be enormous, especially if she were to seek sanctuary with one of his longtime enemies, such as good old Duke Anthony Ulrich of Wolfenbüttel.

No, it was better to stir the pot now so that George stood in her debt when he wore the electoral cap of Hanover.

And she had to stir fast, because Königsmarck's finances were about to change for the better.

A Trip to Saxony

On 27 April 1694, John George IV, Elector of Saxony, died after contracting smallpox whilst nursing his dying mistress[28]. In an extraordinary stroke of luck for Königsmarck, he was succeeded by his younger brother, Augustus[29]. Augustus and Königsmarck had become good friends whilst serving in Flanders together in 1692 and Königsmarck, flush with cash at the time, had been happy to finance his pal's gambling habit whenever Augustus was feeling the pinch. The result was an abiding friendship and a debt of tens of thousands of crowns, which Augustus had not yet repaid.

John George IV's death took everyone by surprise, especially Augustus, but for Königsmarck it was a vital lifeline. Augustus had more money than he could ever spend now and the time seemed right to call in those loans that had been made years earlier. It would be enough to resolve Königsmarck's financial problems and even finance the escape he and Sophia Dorothea dreamed of.

Königsmarck travelled to Dresden to catch up with his friend and tactfully mention those unpaid gambling debts. Augustus was delighted to see him and in the hard-partying court, the two men renewed their acquaintance. Augustus was known for his extravagant lifestyle and he adored excess in all things, from food to furnishings to female company[30]. The atmosphere in Hanover, with its ailing elector and war-stretched coffers, was the polar opposite to the knees-up in Dresden!

Here Königsmarck found himself enjoying the sort of lifestyle that he could no longer afford in Hanover and when Augustus offered him the position of major-general, he accepted. I've no doubt that he took the decision after conferring with Sophia Dorothea, as there's no way he would have said yes without at least discussing the matter with her. Rather, I think, this was the first decisive step that he was able to take towards their future, securing a prestigious and well-paid position safely away from the clutches of Ernest Augustus and George.

In Dresden, Königsmarck once again could enjoy the life that his straitened financial situation in Hanover had been slowly suffocating. Augustus had little love for his late brother and instead of mourning, the court rang with the sound of parties and feasting and Königsmarck was happy to indulge. Back home Sophia Dorothea was still watched and chaperoned, as miserable and trapped as ever, but Königsmarck was enjoying every second of his new-found freedom.

And drinking.

A lot.

Unfortunately, Königsmarck and booze were never happy bedfellows and when he was in his cups, he lost all sense of decorum. Usually it was a cause of embarrassment and nothing more but in Saxony, drunk on wine and fun, he let his mouth run away with him. Like a naughty child, Königsmarck thrived on attention and there was no surer way to get attention than by sharing a few scandalous and gossipy tales of Hanover. Surrounded by an enthralled audience he forgot himself, revelling in the laughter of those who were hanging on his every word.

And somehow, conversation turned to Clara.

There, in the glittering Dresden court, Königsmarck skewered Countess von Platen again and again. He told of her milk baths and her scabrous skin, of her increasingly heavy make- up, of her affair with the elector and how she humiliated him by cavorting with younger, better looking men even as the elderly ruler believed that she was faithful to him alone. He told of his own short affair with Clara and her increasingly desperate efforts to keep him in her control, even telling his audience about her offer of her own daughter's hand in marriage. And finally, if all of that wasn't humiliating enough, he described how Clara hated Sophia Dorothea because she was more accomplished, sensitive and beautiful than the ageing countess could ever hope to be.

And that was before he got started on Melusine and George. He described Melusine as the Electoral Prince's drab, unattractive and grasping mistress and wondered that any man could possibly choose such a creature over Sophia Dorothea. Was it any wonder, asked the loose-lipped count, that the unhappy Electoral Princess was so miserable when she was unwelcome in the court that she would one day preside over? Thank goodness Sophia Dorothea had a friend like Königsmarck in whom she could confide, was his utterly blunt conclusion, even as he spilled those confidences all over Saxony.

And somewhere there, amongst Königsmarck's enthralled audience, a spy was lurking.

Act Three: Prisoner

'It is known that in Queen Anne's time there was much noise about French prophets. A female of that vocation warned George I to take care of his wife, as he would not survive her a year.'[1]

Königsmarck, it seemed, wasn't the only person in Saxony that day who liked to blab because some unknown but mischievous member of his audience couldn't wait to report back to Hanover. Whilst the count was still in Saxony, news of his drunken ramblings had reached the electoral court and landed, unsurprisingly, in Clara's lap. Stung by what he had said about her and salty over being made the subject of such an unflattering portrait, she went to Ernest Augustus to tell him what had happened. By now recovering from his not-so-fatal-after-all illness, the elector listened with increasing annoyance to just how comprehensively Königsmarck had savaged the hand that had been feeding him.

We can safely surmise that Clara would have artfully edited out Königsmarck's claims regarding her legion of young handsome lovers, but what she wouldn't have whitewashed was his declaration that Sophia Dorothea was miserable in the court of Hanover, nor her disdain for the place. Yet Sophia Dorothea wasn't the only one who had reached the end of her tether. She and George argued constantly and this latest embarrassment, courtesy of Königsmarck, was the final straw for both of them.

Though Sophia Dorothea was doing all she could to keep her distance from her husband and George had been perfectly content in the company of his mistress, the news from Dresden changed this unhappy but relatively calm status quo. If Ernest Augustus and Clara were seething at Königsmarck's comments, Melusine was devastated at his unflattering description of her. And if Melusine was devastated, George was furious. Not so long ago he had violently assaulted his wife and now, filled with rage, he did it again.

George burst into Sophia Dorothea's rooms and asked her exactly what she had been saying to Königsmarck and more to the point, exactly what form their relationship really took. Perhaps lent a little courage thanks to her knowledge that her lover was establishing himself - and by extension, her - in Dresden, this time Sophia Dorothea didn't back down. It wasn't her who was the laughing stock of Europe, she retaliated, but George and his father. Everyone knew that Ernest Augustus was Clara's puppet, Sophia Dorothea bellowed, and everyone was laughing behind their hands at the miserable little electoral prince and his 'tall mawkin'. The floodgates had opened and as husband and wife raged back and forth in that apartment in the Leineschloss, it was like a dam bursting.

On and on went the argument, this way and that flew the recriminations. Every grievance, every slight Sophia Dorothea had ever suffered now came flooding out. Just as he had before, George finally tired of fighting with words and flew at his wife, locking his hands around her throat. Fortunately Sophia Dorothea's panicked and desperate gasps brought Eleonore von dem Knesebeck rushing to her aid. Sophia Dorothea was barely conscious as her friend bundled her to safety and this time, it seemed as though there was no brushing it under the carpet.

Ready to depart on a prearranged visit to Berlin, George told Sophia Dorothea that, 'this constraint is too much; on my return I shall write to your father and demand a separation'[2]. Even in her distress, that must have been like sunlight peeking through rainclouds to Sophia Dorothea. She wasn't about to sit in the Leineschloss as everyone discussed her business though, and instead immediately began to pack. Her intention, understandable given the circumstances, was to leave for the safety of Celle. This time, she had already decided that she would never come back.

Sophia Dorothea must have felt as though Christmas had come. All she should have had to do was wait, but Königsmarck's drunken floorshow had driven a coach and horses right through their plans for escape.

Just as the electress had travelled through the night to beg George William for his daughter's hand for her taciturn son, now Sophia Dorothea headed out into the darkness without any thought for her own safety. On arriving in Celle there was no ceremony, only a young woman in distress whose neck was bruised by her own husband's hands. She begged her parents to let her stay and Éléonore, horrified at her daughter's plight, said yes. Imagine Sophia Dorothea's surprise when George William, the devoted father who had always adored her, took the opposing view. He had listened too closely to the counsel of the scheming Bernstorff, the man who had once helped Clara to secure the very marriage that was now falling apart, and Bernstorff told him that Sophia Dorothea must go home to Hanover without delay.

George William was torn between duty to his daughter and loyalty to his brother. Even as he agonised, all he could hear were the rattling sabres of the Danish troops who were still far too close for comfort to Celle. To shelter Sophia Dorothea was to risk alienating Ernest Augustus and his heir, George, and to alienate the current elector and his successor might prove costly if they withdrew Hanover's military support. Celle had once been rich but all of those skirmishes cost money and much as George William loved his daughter, to lose his brother's armed backing could be catastrophic.

Fortunately for everyone, Sophia Dorothea's moonlit flight to safety and the horrible argument that preceded it had left her exhausted. There was no question of her travelling anywhere anytime soon, let alone that same night, and Éléonore summoned a doctor to the bedside of the electoral princess to give the official verdict on her ailing spirits. His diagnosis was one of exhaustion and whatever Bernstorff might have wanted, he found himself usurped by the court physician. What Sophia Dorothea needed was rest, time to recover her health both physically and mentally and to get over the fatigue that had left her reeling.

George William received the doctor's recommendations with a heavy heart and wrote to his brother, informing him that Sophia Dorothea was currently too ill to go home. He assured Ernest Augustus that her absence was a temporary one and that as soon as she was sufficiently recovered, he would ensure that she returned promptly to Hanover. The elector and electress weren't sorry to learn that Sophia Dorothea wouldn't be hurrying back and with George safely out of the way visiting his sister in Berlin, it seemed as though a little distance might be exactly what was needed. Emotions were running high and some time to cool down could do no harm, after all.

In the event it was a couple of months before George William decided that he could delay no longer. Sophia Dorothea begged to be allowed to remain permanently but her father wouldn't hear of it. The two argued bitterly but ultimately, she knew that the die was cast. With a heavy heart, Sophia Dorothea packed for her return journey to Hanover.

Although she had left by night without ceremony, the return of the electoral princess was going to be anything but low key. She was told to go not to the Leineschloss but to Herrenhausen, where her parents-in-law were in residence and would be delighted to receive her. This request was intended to give the impression of a happy, united family, in contrast to what Königsmarck had claimed about her miserable life. Though Sophia Dorothea could be compelled to leave Celle, she couldn't be forced to play happy families and as the Hanoverian court gathered in Hanover to receive their returning princess, everybody waited to see what would happen. Would she play along and do her duty or might she cause a scene? Would there be even more juicy gossip once Sophia Dorothea arrived to her official welcome?

In fact, Sophia Dorothea did something even worse than causing a scene: she blanked the lot of them. As her carriage thundered along the road to Herrenhausen, Ernest Augustus, Sophia, and the entire court assembled amid great pomp to welcome her. The enormous gates of Herrenhausen were opened but at the last second Sophia Dorothea could be seen addressing the coachman and at her command he sped past and headed into the distance, literally leaving the court in the dust.

It was a slap in the face. To so publicly reject the hospitality of the court said more than any words could and everybody knew it. Upon reaching the Leineschloss Sophia Dorothea went straight to her bed and sent word that she would see nobody.

Except, of course, Count Philip Christoph von Königsmarck.

Death Comes to Hanover

Sophia Dorothea's bed-in was less than a week old when Königsmarck returned to Hanover. Both knew that the time to flee had come. Königsmarck had his new position in Dresden so all he had to do was wind up his affairs in Hanover then, one way or another, he would finally be free of the place. Both he and Sophia Dorothea were determined that she would be at his side when he left for good, but they didn't intend to establish themselves as a couple in Saxony, knowing that such an idea would be unthinkable. Instead, they hoped to let the dust settle by seeking shelter for Sophia Dorothea with none other than Duke Anthony Ulrich in Wolfenbüttel. With diplomatic relations between Wolfenbüttel and Hanover non-existent, such a move would be tantamount to treason. The only possible outcome for Sophia Dorothea would be the divorce she so longed for.

When Königsmarck returned to Hanover, where his drunken gossip had made him an unwelcome figure, he intended to stay only as long as it would take to resign his commission in the elector's army and arrange his lover's safe passage to Wolfenbüttel. The clandestine couple knew that now more than ever they had to take care but as we know, they never showed too much common sense and in the summer of 1694, that proved to be a fatal mistake. Literally.

As evening fell on 1 July 1694, Königsmarck took delivery of a letter written in pencil that purported to be from Sophia Dorothea. In it she begged him to come to her rooms after dark and he, as always, obeyed. Usually so fashionable and well turned out, he dressed in a scruffy disguise and at around 11.00 pm, ventured to the Leineschloss. There he discovered that far from summoning him, Sophia Dorothea had not been expecting a visit at all. Upon seeing the letter she told him that she hadn't written it and suspected that it was another of Clara's troublemaking schemes. What followed can only be pieced together from sometimes confusing and often contradictory versions of events given by everyone from Knesebeck to Aurora von Königsmarck and beyond but on one thing all were agreed: Königsmarck was never seen again after that fateful night.

Perhaps one day, by some miracle, the Leineschloss will give up its secrets. Until it does all we can do is draw on the rumours, legends and gossip to construct the most likely narrative of events. And what a story emerges!

By the summer of 1694, Königsmarck's position in Hanover was no longer tenable. Heavily in debt, beset by rumour and gossip and without hope of advancement in the army, he had accepted the position of major-general in the service of the Elector of Saxony. It was a new start for Königsmarck and a desperately needed lifeline, but it also meant that he and Sophia Dorothea needed to make a move. None of this had escaped Clara's attention and when one pairs a fiercely strategic mind with a love of mischief and that seething jealousy that had been a thorn in her side ever since Königsmarck had ended their affair, you have all the ingredients for trouble.

Clara had watched the romance since its beginning and had probably read a fair few of the letters exchanged by Königsmarck and Sophia

Dorothea too, as delays, broken seals and occasionally mislaid missives suggest. She knew that Königsmarck wouldn't abandon his lover in Hanover and she knew also that this would be the perfect opportunity to deal Sophia Dorothea her death blow. She went to Ernest Augustus and told him that Königsmarck and Sophia Dorothea were planning to flee. The embarrassment to Hanover of such a scandal would be immense and if Sophia Dorothea were to be sheltered by Wolfenbüttel, just as Max had been, it would be doubly damaging.

Until then, Ernest Augustus had not seen any reason to censure Königsmarck but if his outburst in Saxony was a step too far, spiriting Sophia Dorothea away was the final straw. As the most likely author of the false letter, Clara knew that the couple was together in Sophia Dorothea's rooms and she promised Ernest Augustus that, if he were to take action now, then he would see for himself that Sophia Dorothea had betrayed her husband. She spun a good tale and the elector agreed that Königsmarck should be detained and questioned about the whole affair, but at this point there was no talk of execution.

As Königsmarck and Sophia Dorothea discussed their plans, one thought assailed the electoral princess and it wasn't excitement for the freedom that now seemed so close. Instead, the reality of departure was starting to bite and she thought only of the children she would be leaving behind, with precious little hope of ever seeing them again once she had burnt her last bridge at Hanover. She needed to say a proper and loving goodbye to her son and daughter. Once that was done, she and Königsmarck would finally be able to leave.

When Königsmarck and Sophia Dorothea said their goodnights, it was with the mutual belief that they would soon be free of the Leineschloss and the elector and the need for stolen liaisons. Sophia Dorothea immediately began to pack. She was determined to be gone by the next dusk and if she hadn't been so concerned for her children, it's likely she and Königsmarck would have left that very night. Their delay was to prove fatal.

The palace was in darkness when Königsmarck stole from Sophia Dorothea's bedroom and crept through the darkened hallways, but not everyone was sleeping. Clara Elisabeth von Meysenburg, Countess of Platen and Hallermund, had secreted herself in a chamber with four loyal and drunken halberdiers, all of them armed to the teeth as they listened for the tell-tale tread of Königsmarck's feet.

When Königsmarck reached the door through which he flitted when he wished to visit his lover, he found it unexpectedly locked. It was then that Clara's henchmen emerged from their hiding place and confronted him. Ernest Augustus had agreed only to have Königsmarck arrested but Clara had no intention of keeping that agreement, she had murder on her mind. Königsmarck had no way out and he knew it. When the four halberdiers attacked, they gave no quarter.

Königsmarck was outnumbered and easily subdued. Bleeding heavily, his last act before he fell unconscious was to beg for Sophia Dorothea's life. Insensible but still alive - just - Königsmarck was dragged into the room where Clara waited. She watched him as impassively as a spider might watch a fly in its web until he regained consciousness. He blinked away the blood that clouded his vision and with his dying breath greeted Clara with a furious oath, recognising only now the magnitude of her wrath. Clara's reply said more than any words ever could. She lifted her ladylike foot and kicked her former lover in the mouth with all her might.

Count Philip Christoph von Königsmarck, the man who had survived wars and disease, who had once soared so very high, who had loved Sophia Dorothea just as she loved him, was dead. With him died all hope of freedom for the Electoral Princess of Hanover.

As Clara stared down at the bloodied, battered corpse of the man she had once taken to her bed, the cold reality of what she had done hit home with the force of a punch. Until that moment, her malice had been confined only to harsh words and scheming but all that had changed. In the space of an evening, she had created the ideal circumstances for murder.

Clara panicked. She had deliberately ignored the elector's instructions to simply apprehend Königsmarck and instead he lay dead, murdered by the countess and her drunken henchmen. There was no way that she could pretend innocence this time.

Usually calm and collected, Clara hurried to Ernest Augustus' rooms. When she arrived she told him an edited version of events, one in which Königsmarck's violent resistance ended in his death. The elector knew too well how badly this could play for him if news of the death reached Saxony or Sweden, let alone the numerous other opponents who had done all they could to prevent Hanover from becoming an electorate. He was furious at Clara for putting him in such a difficult position and for the first time in their long relationship, she found herself not the mistress of her lover, but the object of his ire. Ernest Augustus could rant and rave all he wished but ultimately he had no choice but to plunge deeper into the chaos that had been unleashed in his palace. He told Clara in no uncertain terms to ensure that Königsmarck's body disappeared and with it, all trace of the nobleman's bloody death.

The couple took stock of who knew their secret and as far as they could conclude, there were only six. This number included Clara, Ernest Augustus, and the four halberdiers. Sophia Dorothea and her companion, Eleanore von dem Knesebeck, would know only that Königsmarck had been present in the electoral princess' rooms and subsequently vanished, but any attempt to report his disappearance would simply implicate them. They couldn't raise the alarm without admitting that Sophia Dorothea and Königsmarck had been alone together in her room, which was some small comfort to Clara.

That left the halberdiers as the weakest link in the chain, but they were also the most vulnerable as they weren't witnesses, but the perpetrators. Precious little is known of the four men but Professor Georg Schnath uncovered proof that Duke Anthony Ulrich of Brunswick-Wolfenbüttel heard from some unnamed source in Hanover that one of the killers was a courtier named Don Nicolò Montalbano. Montalbano's salary was 200 thalers but quite out nowhere, not long after Königsmarck disappeared, Ernest Augustus made an unexplained payment of 150,000 thalers to Montalbano. Further smaller payments followed in increments until his death just a few months later; was this money intended to buy a killer's silence?

The other men who killed Königsmarck were named by Schnath as a gluttonous courtier named Stubenvol, Klencke, a respectable diplomat, and Eltz, who eventually became a privy counsellor. Königsmarck had no love for Montalbano or Stubenvol but Klencke and Eltz were respectable men indeed. What drew them into the plot remains a mystery, but Clara always knew how to spin a good yarn when she needed to get someone on side, so it wouldn't have been too much of a challenge for her to convince them to offer their support.

We don't know happened to Königsmarck's body. Nor did Horace Walpole, but it didn't stop him from coming up with a suitably Gothic theory of his own.

'From that moment he disappeared; nor was it known what became of him, till on the death of George I, on his son the new King's first journey to Hanover, some alterations in the palace being ordered by him, the body of Königsmarck was discovered under the floor of the Electoral Princess's dressing-room — the Count having probably been strangled there the instant he left her, and his body secreted. The discovery was hushed up; George II entrusted the secret to his wife, Queen Caroline, who told it to my father; but the King was too tender of the honour of his mother to utter it to his mistress; nor did Lady Suffolk[3] ever hear of it, till I informed her of it several years afterwards. The disappearance of the Count made his murder suspected, and various reports of the discovery of his body have of late years been spread, but not with the authentic circumstances.'[4]

In fact, Königsmarck's body wasn't found under the floor of Sophia Dorothea's dressing room or anywhere else. Quite apart from anything else, there would have been nothing whatsoever to gain from hiding the body in such a place when there was a sprawling palace in which to conceal it, not to mention the fast-moving waters of the Leine river flowing right past its walls.

In the years since Königsmarck's death other theories have been put forward to suggest that the nobleman was walled up, his body covered in quicklime, whilst Thackeray was certain that he had been burned and his ashes carried away on a no doubt swirling and foreboding wind. More likely, I think, Königsmarck's body was weighted and hurled into the Leine where the current swept it far, far away from Hanover.

The Morning After

As day dawned over the Leineschloss, there was no trace of Königsmarck anywhere to be found. Not a drop of spilled blood remained but for those who had been present at the murder, the memory wasn't so easily wiped away.

Whatever became of Königsmarck's body, the next day passed without anyone raising the alarm. He was known to be an impetuous character and spending a night or two away from home wasn't that unusual, so his household would have suspected nothing untoward. Sophia Dorothea was the only person who would have had reason to fear that something was amiss and as the day passed into evening, her jewels packed and her heart set on flight, she wondered what might be the cause of the delay. There was nothing she could do without arousing suspicion so instead she waited, listening out for any sign of the man she loved and would never see again.

Two days after Königsmarck's death his secretary, Hildebrand, visited Marshal Podewils and reported his master's disappearance. Podewils didn't share Hildebrand's fears of foul play and assured him that there was no need to worry, Königsmarck was able to look after himself and would soon be home once more. Hildebrand, who knew all about the dangerous affair between the count and the electoral princess, wasn't convinced. He sent a note to Saxony, letting the elector know of Königsmarck's mysterious absence.

The next morning Hanoverian officials arrived at Königsmarck's house. If Hildebrand hadn't suspected foul play before, by the time they had rifled through Königsmarck's home and seized all his personal letters and paperwork, he was certain that the affair had finally caught up with his boss. He wrote to Aurora and told her that her brother was missing in mysterious circumstances, assuring her that he would send word as soon as there was something to report.

Aurora wasn't about to sit around and do nothing. Instead she wrote to the electors - Ernest Augustus included - and asked if they could offer some assistance in the search for Königsmarck. Banished from Hanover, she went instead to Dresden and appealed for the help of the new elector, Königsmarck's old friend and ally and now his employer. Having already heard from the anxious Hildebrand, Augustus needed no further prompting to open his own investigations. He sent an envoy to Hanover to discover what had become of the count.

Incidentally, though Aurora's efforts to discover her brother's fate were unsuccessful, something else certainly did come of the trip to Dresden. Twelve months later she returned to the court of Augustus, this time as his mistress and eventually, mother to one of his illegitimate children[5].

Sophia Dorothea's first indication that things had gone badly wrong came when her children failed to keep a regular appointment to visit her chambers. When she attempted to go and see them, she was politely informed that Ernest Augustus had requested that she remain in her rooms, without the company of her children. Instead, they would be cared for by the elector. Her worst fears were coming true. The affair had been discovered and her lover had been somehow detained, though at this point she probably believed that he had been imprisoned as there was no reason to suspect foul play.

Rumours of imprisonment were rife at court and they soon began to seep out into neighbouring territories. In Hanover, meanwhile, the papers seized from Königsmarck's rooms were all the evidence that could be needed of intrigue. The coded names and presence of Eleanore von dem Knesebeck's handwriting did nothing to put the elector off the scent. He knew that the letters could only be from Sophia Dorothea, regardless of whose hand had written them, and they were proof of an affair and a planned departure. Simply put, they were proof of treason.

Sophia Dorothea knew nothing of the evidence that had been assembled against her. She remained under unofficial house arrest, unable to leave her rooms and forbidden from speaking to Ernest Augustus, whom she still wrongly believed to be her defender. In fact, Ernest Augustus was anything but that, having seen in her letters how she had mocked the court and her husband, complained about her in-laws and Clara, and bitterly criticised her own father for his refusal to give her an establishment or income of her own.

In Celle, the letters were received with similar horror by George William, who blanched at the evidence of his daughter's wrongdoing. George was far from an ideal husband but Sophia Dorothea was expected to behave in a manner that was beyond reproach, especially when it came to the bedroom. Only her mother, Éléonore, asked for mercy for Sophia Dorothea. She remembered too well how her daughter had railed against the marriage to George and she recalled too the violent quarrels between the couple, as well as Sophia Dorothea's unhappy years under the watchful eye of Clara and the court. She begged George William to help Sophia Dorothea but he refused, furious at what he had read in the letters.

It's a measure of how desperate Éléonore became that she even approached Bernstorff for help, offering him a large bribe if he would plead Sophia Dorothea's case with George William. Bernstorff agreed. He pocketed the money then did precisely nothing, safe in the knowledge that the desperate Éléonore would assume that he was keeping his side of the bargain. In reality it's hard to know what anyone could have done once the letters were public knowledge, but Éléonore was beside herself with worry about her daughter, and willing to do anything to help her.

The woman who had written those letters was doing nothing to help her own case either. Sophia Dorothea raged against her captivity, demanding to be released. All the time she was certain that Königsmarck was alive somewhere, being kept from her. For more than a week she waited, ignorant of her lover's fate and kept from her children. The official explanation for Sophia Dorothea's absence was that she had fallen ill but the gossips had got there first and with Aurora's letters asking for help doing the rounds, it didn't take much imagination to link Sophia Dorothea's indisposition to Königsmarck's sudden and unexplained disappearance.

Sophia Dorothea couldn't be held indefinitely and finally it was decided that she should be questioned. The man chosen to perform this duty was Count von Platen, whose own wife was responsible for the death of Königsmarck. It is entirely possible that he knew full well what Clara had done but even if he didn't, the cunning first minister would never give Sophia Dorothea even the slightest bit of slack. By now everyone knew what Sophia Dorothea thought of Clara thanks to the scathing content of her letters but faced with Platen she wasn't apologetic or embarrassed. Instead, two weeks of silence had transformed the electoral princess' anguish into rage.

Sophia Dorothea demanded that Platen explain the reason for her treatment and he answered unflinchingly. She was being kept in detention, he replied, because she had betrayed her husband with Königsmarck and they had the evidence to prove it. It was Platen who told her that Königsmarck was dead, killed whilst resisting arrest as he left Sophia Dorothea's rooms on 1 July. I suspect that he relished performing that particular duty, which roundly yanked the rug out from beneath the princess' feet.

Confronted with the death of her lover, Sophia Dorothea's anger deserted her and she was overwhelmed by grief. She fainted clean away. When she regained her senses, Sophia Dorothea screamed that Königsmarck had been murdered and all the time, Platen stood by and coldly watched. She must understand, he explained, that this was no trifling matter. Sexual indiscretion on the princess' part could introduce a bastard into the House of Hanover, a cuckoo into the electoral nest.

Platen's words clearly weren't intended to bring Sophia Dorothea anything but misery and by the time he left, she was despairing. In fact, she became so insensible with grief that there was a genuine fear that she might throw herself out of the window or take her life in some other manner and Ernest Augustus had Sophia Dorothea placed on suicide watch, believing that she was planning to do herself harm.

After all of those heartfelt, florid letters, the protestations that Sophia Dorothea or Königsmarck's life would be over were they ever to part, the worst had happened and Sophia Dorothea was alone. Worse still, the letters had ensured that virtually everyone was bound to turn against her thanks to the words she hadn't expected anyone to see other than Königsmarck. Who hasn't criticised a parent or a spouse in the heat of anger and emotion before immediately forgetting and moving on with life? It's hardly news that in-laws don't always get along and the insults Sophia Dorothea wrote in her missives were nothing more serious than a million family arguments that happen all over the globe every day, but this was no ordinary family. The House of Hanover was grievously offended and something must be done.

George offered one last olive branch to his loathed wife and Sophia Dorothea was given her final get out clause. If she were to swear her fidelity to George and resume her wifely duties at court as well as in the bedroom, then all might still be mended. Unsurprisingly she refused, stating that, 'if what I am accused of it true, I am unworthy of his bed; and if the accusation is false, he is unworthy of me. I will not accept his offers.'[6] Instead she asked to be allowed to go home to her parents in Celle, a free woman.

Whilst she remained married to George, Sophia Dorothea couldn't live in Celle as though nothing had happened and besides, George William didn't want her under his roof. Likewise she didn't want to remain in Hanover and the longer she did, the louder the rumours became. Instead Ernest Augustus decided that the safest thing was to send her to Ahlden House, which lay in territory controlled by Celle, and tell the world that the decision had been made by Sophia Dorothea herself. Count von Platen wrote to Bernstorff that, 'as to the proposition of suggesting [that Sophia Dorothea] may declare, in order to save appearances, that she will not, and cannot, live with the Prince, and therefore has begged leave to retire before his return here, we consider it desirable to spread such a rumour abroad, but not to suggest to the Princess that she should say it.'

127

It would be cleaner for all concerned, he decided, as 'the departure of Madame la Princesse Electorale cannot possibly pass for desertion, as she wishes to take all her belongings and attendants with her.'

By now Königsmarck had been missing for a fortnight. All at Hanover were anxious to draw the affair to a close without linking Sophia Dorothea's name to the missing count in any sort of official capacity. With interest all over Europe showing no sign of fizzling out, something had to be done soon if only to put a lid on the fervent speculation about the count's fate. Ten days after Platen wrote to Bernstorff regarding the planned move to Ahlden, George Stepney, William III's envoy to Dresden, wrote to James Cresset, his opposite number in Hanover, and neatly summed up the situation.

'I have great curiosite to know what piece of mischief has been brewing at Hanover. If you dare not trust it at length, I must beg you to satisfy me in Cypher, as likewise with the particulars of your Princess's ruine. Amours are fatal in these parts; wee have had a scene of them and may hereafter have more the like nature. But at present the Tragedy is removed to your Courts, and I fear Daggers and poyson will be as familiar among you as they are in Italy. Your Princes have often been there and may have learned the humour of the country of despatching people without Noise. A servant or two of Count Königsmarck run frequently betwixt this place and Hanover [...] seeking out their master, but have no tidings. Our Elector sent one of his Adjutants, Mr. Bannier (a swede likewise) to Hannover, I believe with a design to stopp the blow if it was not yet given. But I suppose the Corps by this time is in the common shore, and our Elector by the accident has cleared the debt of 30 thousand R he had lost to him two years ago at play.

I have been told his sister [Aurora] raves like Cassandra and will know what is become of her brother; but at Hannover they answer like Cain, that they are not her brother's keeper and that the Body should be found (which I believe as little as that of Moses), yet the circumstances of the murder will be left as much in the dark as the manner of despatching Sir Edmonbury Godfrey has been. He [Königsmarck] was not recommended to be my Mr. Stratford. I knew him in England, at Hamburg, in Flanders, and at Hanover for a dissolute debauchee whom I would always have avoided. By chance I ate with him here at Count Frizews and our new privy counsellor Haxthausen, and by chance likewise they did suppe with me, whereas they were invited to Mr. Bomeburgh's who too late remembered it was a fish-night and so shifted off his own company onto me. This is all I have had to do with the spark, and if he has been as black as we think he is, his Fate (be what it will) is not to be pitied.'[7]

And if Königsmarck's fate wasn't one to be envied, Sophia Dorothea's was to be no picnic either.

Ahlden House was the perfect place in which to secrete an unwanted, unfaithful spouse. Situated on the Aller, 40 miles from the Leineschloss and 25 miles from her birthplace in Celle, it was grand enough to be respectable but not so grand as to be opulent. Here in a little-known village, away from the social whirl she had once enjoyed, the elector and his son hoped that Sophia Dorothea would be forgotten.

The Aftermath

It wasn't only Sophia Dorothea whose marriage was now in crisis. George wasn't implicated in Königsmarck's disappearance but it couldn't fail to have an impact on him, especially now his wife was very publicly living elsewhere. Though he had thundered and threatened separation when he left for Berlin, George found now that things had moved on apace without the need for legal intervention and across Europe, people were talking. Exactly what had happened between the couple remained a mystery but that didn't stop the gossip and with Königsmarck's disappearance, the triangle was a fairly easy one to map out.

In a hopeless effort to stem the tide of rumour, Hanover's envoys were instructed to meet questions about the situation with a wall of placatory falsehoods. Königsmarck's name wasn't to be mentioned, certainly not in connection to Sophia Dorothea, and if it seemed that the marriage was in trouble, that was entirely the wrong impression. Instead the electoral princess had simply elected to spend some time at Ahlden, and there was nothing more to it than that. It was an unconvincing effort at best.

> 'The Princess at first displayed only some coldness towards her husband, but Fraulein von Knesebeck by degrees inspired her with such dislike to him that she begged from her father permission to return to her parents' home. Her father was displeased, and warned the Princess to place confidence in her husband. After that she paid her father a visit at Brockhausen; but when he learnt that the Prince was intending to make a journey to Berlin to see his sister, he sent his daughter back to Hanover with further admonitions that she should speak with her husband before his departure. But her dislike of her husband was so intensified by the machinations of Fraulein von Knesebeck that she determined not to await his return from Berlin. As soon as his arrival was imminent, she withdrew again from Hanover to her father. He, however, sent messengers to meet her on the way to forbid her coming to Celle, and insisted on her either returning, or withdrawing for the present to the magistrate's house at Ahlden, which lay on the way. The Princess chose the latter course; but her corrupter, Fraulein von Knesebeck, was arrested at the wish of the Duke George William.'

Stepney knew better than this official line and noted darkly that, 'tis an even lay that they have used him little better than his Brother did Esquire Thinn'[8] and in the dark shadow cast by this sly reference to the murder of Thomas Thynne, we learn exactly what people were saying about Königsmarck's disappearance. His death was an open secret; all that was left was to ascertain who was responsible for it. There was no possibility of Clara or those who had wielded the halberds ever facing justice though. Blanket denial was the order of the day.

In Dresden, Aurora had successfully awakened Augustus' concerns for his newly-promoted, newly-vanished major-general. He sent his envoy, Johann Bannier, to Hanover with express instructions to discover the truth behind the matter, and Bannier was determined not to return without a satisfactory answer. Even as Bannier quizzed Ernest Augustus, his opposite number in Saxony was smoothing over the elector's concerns there, assuring Augustus that everything that could be done was being done, alas to no avail.

In England, King William had had enough. News reached him that the sibling rulers of Hanover and Celle had grown tired and offended thanks to the tenacity of the envoy from Dresden, who seemed determined to suggest that they were implicated in the disappearance of Königsmarck. The Grand Alliance rested on a knife edge thanks to the mystery and one wrong word might bring it down, especially if Saxony and Hanover couldn't declare a truce.

Such intrigues would only serve to further undermine the already teetering alliance and William was sure that nothing good could come out of further investigations by any party. With the monarch's encouragement, Stepney tactfully asked Augustus whether he considered himself satisfied with Ernest Augustus' assurances that he had no idea what had become of the missing Swede. To everyone's relief - other than Aurora's, perhaps - Augustus confirmed that he was. It was likely that Königsmarck had met with mischief from a private party, he declared, and there was little more that he or his counterpart in Hanover could do about that.

Stepney recorded the end of the confrontation between the two electorates. He observed that things seemed to settle down in Dresden once Hanover confirmed that Königsmarck was likely dead, even though they didn't know who had dealt the fatal blow.

> 'The Elector of Saxony seemed very moderate after this answer, as if he doubted not the truth of what had been offered and replyed, only that he hoped as an instance of friendship that ye Elector of Hannover would give him notice as soon as he should learn any tidings of Count Coningsmark [sic], and I believe here that ye affair will end without causing any breach betwixt ye two Electors.'[9]

And there the official investigations into the death of Königsmarck ended.

Divorce

Sophia Dorothea left for her new home of Ahlden on 17 July, little suspecting that she would remain there - give or take a few weeks - for the remaining thirty years of her life. This time she didn't have her confidante, Eleonore von dem Knesebeck, with her, because the lady-in-waiting had been detained in Hanover by Count von Platen. He was sure that she'd spill the beans on exactly what had been going on between the electoral princess and her lover, and she couldn't do that from the relatively distant Ahlden.

Platen had badly underestimated the loyal Knesebeck though and even under heavy interrogation, she refused to throw her former mistress under the wheels of that particular carriage. Platen was determined to put the blame for the collapse of the electoral heir's marriage on Sophia Dorothea and what better charge could there be than one of adultery, the very sin that could bring a bastard into the line of succession? He had the letters and he had circumstantial gossip but what he didn't have was an eye witness. Though Eleonore von dem Knesebeck could have blown the lid off the whole thing, she remained silent even under the provocation of that official dispatch from Hanover which had blamed her for whipping up a little marital discord into a tsunami. Platen swiftly realised that if he was going to incriminate Sophia Dorothea, then nobody's testimony would be more damning that that of the banished electoral princess herself.

Separated from her children, with the man she loved dead and her father reluctant to indulge her any further, Sophia Dorothea could hardly have been lower. Platen exploited her despair to play his masterstroke and suggested that, should she admit to having deserted her husband, he might be able to work things in Sophia Dorothea's favour. She would be given an allowance by her father, the run of Ahlden and, she assumed, her freedom.

She assumed wrong.

All of Europe believed that Sophia Dorothea had sought to leave George and chosen Ahlden as the place of her seclusion but in fact the restrictions placed on her there were suffocating. George William still hoped that his daughter would find her life so intolerable that she would run back to her husband and his brother, Ernest Augustus, certainly would have found this the easiest solution. In order to ensure that Sophia Dorothea found little to recommend life at Ahlden, George William issued a set of instructions regarding her care.

> '1. Since it is my intention that my daughter should remain at Ahlden, and have no communication, either by letter or other means, with any one whatsoever until

she returns to her duties with the Electoral Prince, her consort, the Seigneur de la Fortière will make himself acquainted with these wishes of mine and what I have ordered, as I do by this present. He is not to convey, nor permit to be conveyed by others to my daughter, any letters except such as come with an order signed by my hand; and in like manner he is not to dispatch, nor allow to be dispatched, any letter of my daughter's except with express permission from me.

2. In conformity with this order, the Seigneur de la Fortière will instruct the women, valets, and other domestics in attendance on my daughter and all who enter the castle, that these who have, or receive, letters for any one whatsoever in, or out of, the castle must place them in the hands of the Seigneur de la Fortière on pain of death.

3. All letters which come for any of the servants, or which are sent by any on their business, will likewise be given to the Seigneur de la Fortière, and read by him, before being allowed to pass; and those which are allowed to go must be stamped with his seal. If the Seigneur de la Fortière finds the slightest cause for suspicion in them, he will send them direct to me.

4. The Seigneur de la Fortière can have all persons searched by the officer or soldiers of the guard who give him the slightest cause to suspect them of being implicated in bringing forbidden messages or letters.

5. Except those at Ahlden in attendance on my daughter, no one else will enter the castle without my express permission; and the above-mentioned servants are to have no conversation with any strangers — that is to say, with any others but those of the household and people of Ahlden — except in the presence of the Seigneur de la Fortière or of some one commissioned by him for that purpose; and the Seigneur de la Fortière will give orders that as soon as strangers arrive in the said Ahlden he shall be immediately informed of the fact.

6. The women and other attendants on my daughter will not go out of the castle without the Seigneur de la Fortière's permission, and the remainder of the servants will only enter the castle at fixed hours to perform their duties, and will go away again as soon as they are done.

7. My daughter will only leave the castle to take a walk, if she wishes, in the garden between the two moats, and then she must be accompanied by the Seigneur de la Fortière.

8. If my daughter wishes to take her meals in the salon outside her rooms, she will have permission to do so, and the persons whose business it is to be in waiting, and the footmen will attend at these meals; but the Seigneur de la Fortière will always be present, and, after rising from table, everybody will leave my daughter except the lady-in-waiting and her chamber attendants.

9. The Seigneur de la Fortière will have the power to require the officer of the guard, in virtue of the orders I have given him for that purpose, to adopt strong measures to ensure the exact execution and observance of the above, as far as such may be necessary."

For Sophia Dorothea, all of these restrictions were preferable to living with George. If she could endure just as long as it took to officially end the marriage, then she might one day taste freedom again. She held the Platens and the court of Hanover responsible for the murder of Königsmarck and under no circumstances did she intend to return to that hated place. Her lover might not be at her side anymore, but still she had her sights set firmly on escape.

Sophia Dorothea's spirits were already low when Bernstorff arrived from Celle to inform her that the facts in the case of her relationship with Königsmarck were now known to both courts. She hit back, claiming that the evidence was all circumstantial and that she had done nothing whatsoever to be ashamed of, a version of events that Knesebeck further supported during her interrogation. In assuming the moral high ground so forcefully, Sophia Dorothea achieved nothing whatsoever and her denial simply wasn't credible, no matter how hard she clung to it. The letters weren't innocent missives of courtly love and fine feelings, but of a couple who were locked in mutual need, raw in emotion and dependency. To claim no sexual intimacy had taken place was a lie, but the price Königsmarck and Sophia Dorothea paid for that intimacy was absurdly high.

A consistorial court (an ecclesiastical court with jurisdiction over moral affairs) was convened in Hanover to hear the divorce case, manned by an equal share of officials from Celle and Hanover. The order of the day was to make the divorce as by the book as possible - albeit with no mention of Königsmarck - and to draw up a workable future plan for Sophia Dorothea. Ultimately it was agreed that the continued care of the electoral princess would be the responsibility of both her father and her soon to be ex-father-in-law. Both would share the job of approving her household staff and she would be paid an annuity of eight thousand thalers, which would go up by fifty per cent when George William died and would be increased by a further six thousand thalers when Sophia Dorothea reached 40. She would be given Ahlden but her valuable inheritance would not revert to her. Instead it would be given directly to George, just as it would have done had the couple remained wed.

On 1 September, the Duke of Celle and the Elector of Hanover signed the agreement and Sophia Dorothea was given one last chance to return to George. She refused and as September drew to a close, she sent a letter which made her wishes starkly clear.

> 'Since our illustrious husband, George Lewis, Crown Prince of Hanover, has caused to be delivered to the matrimonial court in Hanover constituted to try this case by our father and father-in-law, a complaint of desertion against us, and has requested a complete separation of marriage between our husband and us, as we have learned from this complaint, and a communication from the court that made it known to us; and since our lord and father has sent to us his president and grand marshal of the court, von Bulow, at this place, that we might make known what we thought best, according to our comprehension respecting such complaint of desertion, and that we should instruct for that purpose the counsellor of the court Rudolph Thies, in order to convey our declaration

to the said matrimonial court for its information, leaving the circumstances mentioned by the attorney of our lord and husband undisturbed. We declare, for the rest, as we well understand our intention, and in accordance with the contents of the aforesaid complaint, have well and freely considered it, that we still adhere to our oft repeated resolution never to cohabit matrimonially with our husband, and that we desire nothing so much as that separation of marriage requested by our husband may take place.'

With nothing more to be said Sophia Dorothea was brought to Lauenau, which stood on Hanoverian soil, in preparation for her turn before the divorce court. Though the thought of being so close to Hanover chilled her she consented, convinced that once the divorce was final, she would be free to go back to Celle or anywhere else she wished.

Clara, you may notice, had fallen suspiciously silent once the reality of Königsmarck's death had hit home. It was the first time she had found herself on the wrong side of Ernest Augustus and in terms of her place at court, it was catastrophic. She had intended nothing but mischief and the ruination of Sophia Dorothea, but instead she had achieved something far worse. Her rival was certainly removed from the scene but Clara had become damaged goods too, tainted with the suspicious whiff of murder. Ill health had ravaged her lover and as his health failed so too did her influence. She was swiftly becoming yesterday's woman.

The countess and Sophia Dorothea never met again, though Sophia Dorothea never forgot her enemy. When she took the sacrament at Lauenau in the presence of Count von Platen, he met her claims of continued fidelity with a cool, knowing smile that said, *we all know better*. Far from being embarrassed, Sophia Dorothea asked whether the count would invite his wife to make the same oath. The minister's smile vanished.

Sophia Dorothea believed that she stood on the brink of freedom but her legal advisor, Rudolph Thies, thought it more likely that this was the edge of the precipice. Rather than rush the divorce, he counselled her to consider less extreme options first, but she was set on her path. Given one last chance to recant her request for a divorce, she did quite the opposite.

'Now we [Sophia Dorothea] give the circumstances mentioned by the attorney of our Consort Louis, in the charge of desertion brought against us, their due place; but we cannot refrain from again adding that we adhere persistently to the resolution, once drawn up and constantly affirmed, that we will not, and cannot, ever again live in conjugal relations with our Consort Louis, Duke of Brunswick and Lüneburg, Prince Electoral, and we will therefore accept the verdict of the court on the matter.'

Though Sophia Dorothea knew that a divorce would mean that she and her children would no longer live under the same roof, she hadn't considered the long-term implications of that. Custody of the youngsters would certainly be given to their father, but Sophia Dorothea didn't fully grasp the possibility that they might never meet again. Likewise, if she thought divorce would give her the freedom to marry again one day and to find happiness, she was wrong. Though her mother put up a strong defence for remarriage, Count von Platen pointed out to George William that Sophia Dorothea's inheritance had already been pledged to her husband and even formed the basis of the unification of Hanover and Celle. Should she remarry and have further children, they would be within their rights to challenge for their portion of the duchy of Celle. Any such allowance for remarriage was merely sowing the seeds of future catastrophe.

There was no comeback to that and Éléonore's complaints ceased, though she was devastated for her daughter. The unhappy marriage limped to an end on 28 December 1694, with all marital ties formally and eternally severed.

'In the matrimonial suit of the illustrious Prince George Louis, Electoral Prince of Hanover, against his consort, the illustrious Princess Sophie Dorothea, etc., we, constituted president and judges of the Matrimonial Court of the Electorate and Duchy of Brunswick-Lüneburg, declare and pronounce judgement.

After attempts have been tried and have failed to settle the matter amicably, and in accordance with the documents and verbal declarations of the Princess and other detailed circumstances, we agree that her continued denial of matrimonial duty and cohabitations is well founded, and consequently that it is to be considered as an intentional desertion. In consequence whereof we have considered sentence, and now declare the ties of matrimony to be entirely dissolved and annulled.

Since in similar cases of desertion it has been permitted to the innocent party to re-marry, while the other is forbidden, the same judicial power will be exercised in the present instance in favour of His Serene Highness the Electoral Prince.'

Sophia Dorothea had been found guilty. She would never be allowed to marry again.

A Princess in Prison

Just one day after the court gave its verdict, Hanover held its annual celebratory carnival. Alone at Lauenau, meanwhile, Sophia Dorothea had nothing but time on her hands, empty days and long nights to think of what had once been and what she had lost. She had envisioned divorce not as an end but as a beginning, a chance to return to Celle and grieve for her lover as she waited to be reunited with her children. Instead her father's court remained closed to her, with George William still reeling from what he saw as his daughter's despicable behaviour. After the comings and goings of Hanoverian ministers and advisors who had divorce business to discuss, her world had grown silent and in that silence, the grief was thunderous. Grief for her lover, for her children, and, quite naturally, for herself. Not even 30-years-old, she had been through enough misery and drama for a woman twice her age. Her health collapsed and she took to her bed, as did another woman who had once glittered.

Clara von Platen had plenty of time to reflect too. Gossip about her part in the sorry affair began to gather pace as quickly as Ernest Augustus began to lose his health and her once unassailable position grew weaker. She was officially uninvolved but in the hothouse world of the chattering court, her name was on everyone's lips. Over the years of her unofficial reign Clara had spun a web of intrigue and malice that had caught many of her peers in its strands. How they must have relished her fall from grace. The constant whispering and gossip wore her down and her own health grew weak, sending this once powerful woman into seclusion. She was fading fast.

Once the mistress who wielded vast power over her lover's lands, Clara was a siren no more. Milk baths could only go so far in holding back the ravages of syphilis and even Clara's liberal layers of slap could no longer hide the scars of the disease. Blind and disfigured, she thrashed in her bed like the wicked witch of a child's story, raving and tormented by unseen demons. Thackeray believed that Königsmarck's unquiet spirit was among those figures that came to taunt the old countess and some claim that she confessed to the murder in the last hours of her life, desperate to save her soul. Whatever secrets Clara possessed went to the grave with her on 30 January 1700, forever silenced.

But amid all the unhappiness, one person was still fighting for Sophia Dorothea. Éléonore never abandoned her daughter and chief amongst her priorities was getting Sophia Dorothea away from the Hanoverian territory of Lauenau. She petitioned Hanover to have her daughter removed and in February 1695, Sophia Dorothea was taken from Lauenau and returned to Ahlden. In her new home she was given the title of Duchess of Ahlden, a far cry from the rank of electress and queen that might otherwise have been hers. But at least she was free of Hanover.

At Ahlden, Sophia Dorothea was still kept under the watch of a Celle nobleman, the Seigneur de la Fortière[10]. He was charged with monitoring her movements and vetting all correspondence whether incoming or outgoing. This applied to Sophia Dorothea's visitors and household too, all of whom were required to have their correspondence and visitors approved by Sophia Dorothea's minder. He walked alongside her if she strolled in the grounds, her closest and most unwelcome companion from the early days of her confinement. In fact, though George and the court of Hanover have long since been labelled as the jailers of Sophia Dorothea, this wasn't strictly the case. The divorce agreement contained no instructions on where Sophia Dorothea could be confined, nor did Hanover have any right to censure her movements.

Yet a completely free Sophia Dorothea, able to roam where she chose and spread whatever trouble she liked, posed a threat to Hanover. With its status as an electorate far from popular with some of the other electors,

Ernest Augustus couldn't afford for his former daughter-in-law to get cosy with his enemies. For this reason, he had already prevailed upon George William to agree that Sophia Dorothea would remain at Ahlden which, as her father, he had the right to do. As far as the world was concerned, dark forces were massed against the princess and unknown enemies were plotting to kidnap her, so official word was that she was being confined for her own good. This was a lie, but even George William was taken in by his brother's tales of would-be kidnappers circling Ahlden. To further prove the falsehood, every now and then a few armed men were sent to ride through Ahlden as though casing the joint. A report of their movements would be sent to George William, just in case he might be considering bringing his daughter back into the fold at Celle.

Ahlden House didn't serve merely to confine Sophia Dorothea, but also to define her new role as the Duchess of Ahlden. Even as Eleonore von dem Knesebeck was confined to a dank fortress and erased from the collective Hanoverian memory, Sophia Dorothea's cage was a sumptuously gilded one. She had a considerable retinue of staff at her disposal[11], all of whom were naturally expected to keep a close eye on her and report anything suspicious and eventually, it was the management of this staff that drew Sophia Dorothea out of her misery. In order to keep up the fiction that she had requested this new life, she was given the rights to administer the territory of Ahlden and did so with increasing confidence, discovering the joys of philanthropy as she helped the poor of the district. In fact, her charitable nature became so prevalent that Sophia Dorothea was soon as popular in Ahlden as she had been during her youth in Celle, a fact that must have been like a sharp splinter in George's side.

Don't be fooled into thinking that Sophia Dorothea's money all went to the poor, however. Far from it. Though hidden away at Ahlden, she never stopped dressing like the princess she was and she draped herself in jewels, with diamonds glittering in her dark hair, her body clad in the finest gowns even if there were few present who might appreciate them. A visitor to Ahlden years after her death wrote that, 'Local tradition among the peasants of Ahlden still hands down the picture of the mysterious great lady of the castle always beautifully dressed, and with diamonds gleaming in her dark hair, galloping up and down the road, followed by an escort of cavalry with drawn swords.' Yet her liberty wasn't her own and she was desperate for freedom. Eventually she was told by those in the know that if she obeyed every rule and proved to Ernest Augustus that she could behave, she'd probably be free sooner rather than later. Sophia Dorothea was so desperate to show her compliance that when her apartments caught fire, she refused to flee without a signed order from the governor permitting her to leave. Instead she paced the hallways of the smoke-filled wing, clutching her jewels to her bosom until the official permission finally arrived.

Sophia Dorothea ran her household like the proverbial well-oiled machine and was permitted to hold regular levees with members of the local clergy and carefully vetted dignitaries. Of course she wasn't allowed to return any of the visits, but at least it was an opportunity to see some new faces, even it was a far cry from her passionate liaisons with Königsmarck. In fact, the only person that Sophia Dorothea really wanted to see was her mother, but even this was forbidden. Though they wrote constantly to one another, Platen and Bernstorff used Éléonore's long-standing friendship with Duke Anthony Ulrich to suggest that the latter might attempt mischief if Sophia Dorothea were allowed to see her mother in private. Better to keep them at arm's length, the scheming minister told the pliable George William.

At first Sophia Dorothea was kept within the castle walls and forbidden even to attend the local church, but as time passed, the restrictions began to lessen. She was given permission to go to the small church just beyond the limits of her estate and took solace there, even going to so far as to make a gift of an organ to the congregation. An agreed route for carriage outings was drawn up too, with Sophia Dorothea permitted to travel six miles along one road. When she reached a stone bridge, she had to turn back. There was no chance of escape. She was always accompanied by guards and even if she kept on travelling, whipping her horses into a frenzy, where would she go? No dashing soldier was waiting to carry her to safety now.

And what of that other friend, her oldest confidante, Eleonore von dem Knesebeck? Knesebeck had been held in prison in Hanover since shortly after the disappearance of Königsmarck. She had then endured Platen's ceaseless questioning before being bundled off to the distant fortress of Scharzfels, as though she had never existed at all.

Though Sophia Dorothea's place of confinement was certainly more comfortable than Knesebeck's, her friend's term of imprisonment was to prove much shorter. For months Knesebeck's family sought to discover where she had been locked away and eventually they discovered that she was at Scharzfels, where she had kept her sanity by covering the walls of her dank cell with charcoal writings and prayers, telling her story as she dreamed of freedom.

Once again it was Duke Anthony Ulrich who saved the day. He sent a representative disguised as a builder to the fortress, with instructions to bring the lady to safety. Three years after she had been imprisoned, the faux builder lifted Knesebeck out of her cell via a rope dropped through a hole in the ceiling and carried her to sanctuary in Wolfenbüttel. She never recovered the property she had left behind in Hanover but eventually returned to service, this time as the lady-in-waiting of Sophia Dorothea's only daughter, by then the Queen in Prussia.

For those same three years, the unflinchingly obedient Sophia Dorothea clung to the hope that Ernest Augustus, who had once shown her such favour, would let her go home to Celle or even see the children she had been kept from. Her hopes were shattered in 1698 when the old elector died and his son, George, took over at the top. Always petulant and ill-humoured, there was no way that he would grant her any concessions whatsoever and Sophia Dorothea knew it. She wanted nothing from him other than the right to see her children and three days after Ernest Augustus died, Sophia Dorothea wrote to her former husband and begged for the right to embrace her son and daughter.

'I have the honour to write to Your Highness to assure you that I take a real share in your grief at the death of the Elector your father, and I pray God that He may console you, that He may bless your reign with His most precious favours, and that He may console Your Highness with every form of prosperity, These are prayers that I shall make every day of my life for you, and I shall always regret having displeased you. I beg you to grant me pardon for my past faults, as I still entreat you herewith on my knees with all my heart. My sorrow for them is so keen and so bitter that I cannot express it. The sincerity of my repentance should obtain pardon from Your Highness; and if to crown your favour you would permit me to see and embrace our children, my gratitude for such longed-for favours would be infinite, as I desire nothing so earnestly as this, and I should be content to die afterwards. I send a thousand prayers for your preservation and good health.'

It would be false to claim that Sophia Dorothea had been the most attentive mother in Hanover but there's no reason to believe that she was anything other than loving. In fact, both of the children remained devoted to her even after she had been banished, and the exile of Sophia Dorothea was one of the many wrongs that contributed to the bitter relationship between George and their son, George Augustus. Her letter was a waste of time though, as was a similar plea that she sent to Sophia, the dowager electress. Neither she nor George were minded to grant any wish of Sophia Dorothea. Even George William, grieving for his brother, remained determined to do all he could to protect the electorate that Ernest Augustus had worked so hard to establish. If that meant Sophia Dorothea remained at Ahlden, so be it. As a sweetener, George raised Éléonore's allowance from eight thousand thalers to twelve but if he thought this would buy her loyalty he was wrong, for she valued her daughter more than any amount of money.

There was one concession that George was grudgingly willing to grant. He agreed that Éléonore could visit Sophia Dorothea at Ahlden, but her constant pleas to see her children fell on deaf ears. Little did she know that in Hanover, they weren't even allowed to speak her name.

In 1700 Sophia Dorothea was given a temporary respite from her prison when the first sabres began to rattle in what would become the War of the Spanish Succession. French troops marched into Hanoverian territory and as far as Éléonore was concerned, they posed a threat to her daughter. In fact, the chance of the soldiers making an assault on Ahlden was virtually zero, but Éléonore played up the risk. She pointed out that Sophia Dorothea was the mother of the likely future king of England and would make a fine prisoner and bargaining chip for the French. Though George wasn't happy, he didn't argue the point and in Spring 1700, Sophia Dorothea travelled through the night to Celle.

The Duchess of Ahlden's return to her childhood home was without fanfare and the mere blink of an eye in the long years of her captivity. Even when the danger from the French troops had passed, Éléonore did all she could to keep her daughter with her. She spoke of Sophia Dorothea's ill health, claiming that she was far too sick to travel, and she couldn't reasonably say when she would be recovered. George William, who had refused to see Sophia Dorothea, knew that this situation couldn't be allowed to continue. With George and Bernstorff putting pressure on him he eventually told his wife that enough was enough and Sophia Dorothea, all hope lost, was sent back to Ahlden.

Ahlden Life

'On Tuesday morning about one of the Clock, departed this life his Highness *William,* Duke of *Gloucester* at *Windsor*, leaving the court and the whole Nation under unspeakable grief for that great loss.'[12]

In the summer of 1700, as Sophia Dorothea was doing all she could to prolong her stay in Celle, Prince William, Duke of Gloucester, died. He was the only surviving son of Anne, the heir to the English throne, and with his death Parliament grudgingly accepted that things in the English court had to change. William III had no children of his own and Anne, despite seventeen pregnancies, had no other living offspring. Though only 35-years-old and married to Prince George of Denmark, all those pregnancies had taken their toll on her health and the chance that she would give birth to a healthy heir was negligible.

With the possibility of one of the Roman Catholic Stuart family lodging a claim to the throne in the years to come, it was decided that action should be taken. The result was the 1701 Act of Settlement. The act enshrined the line of succession in law and ruled that, if neither William nor Anne were to have any children, then the English crown would be inherited by the closest living Protestant relative. That Protestant was Sophia, the ageing mother of George, and it more or less guaranteed that George himself would one day be crowned king after her death.

What had once been mere expectation was now official.

A grand gathering was held in Hanover to celebrate this episode of good fortune but in Ahlden, Sophia Dorothea languished. By this point, her mother was a regular visitor with news of the children she had not seen for years and Sophia Dorothea took delight in hearing of them as they grew up. In the years that followed, a rumour spread that a young and desperate George Augustus once gave his hunting party the slip and rode at full gallop to Ahlden, where he tried and failed to swim across the river Aller to reach his mother. On his return to Hanover, a furious George read his son the riot act, forbidding him to ever mention his mother again.

This tear-jerking episode is most likely a work of fiction, one more romantic interlude in a life that had once been filled with them. Now it was occupied instead with worship and administration, with diamonds and finery that few would ever see. But Sophia Dorothea would see them, and even if she were no longer an Electoral Princess, she was determined to behave like one.

George William, meanwhile, had remained stubbornly committed to his refusal to ever lay eyes on his daughter again, but as the years passed and he grew more old and frail, he began to wonder at the wisdom of his decision. By now in his eighties, George William amended his will to ensure that Sophia Dorothea would be more than cared for in the event of his death and in Éléonore's will, she was the heiress to a vast fortune. Because George William's duchy of Celle would become the property of George upon his death, George William also ensured that his wife would have a home to call her own if he predeceased her, bequeathing her his lodge at Wienhausen and a newly constructed property in Lüneburg. All of this, along with a fortune in cash, would be Sophia Dorothea's one day. Ironically, the forsaken Duchess of Ahlden was on track to become of the wealthiest women on the continent.

Perhaps the death of Ernest Augustus and events in England gave George William pause for thought and no doubt he felt the years passing keenly, because after a decade of estrangement, his thoughts turned more and more to the daughter he had not seen for so long. Eventually he made plans to join Éléonore on one of her trips to Ahlden but even now, years after Sophia Dorothea could be of any political importance, Bernstorff fretted at the thought of a reconciliation. When George William wouldn't be persuaded against the visit, Bernstorff asked instead if he would at least delay a little. With a shooting trip already planned, George William agreed.

In 1705, still intending to reconcile with Sophia Dorothea once his hunting holiday was done, George William went to Wienhausen. There he caught a cold and, as colds were wont to do for men of 81 years of age in the early eighteenth century, it soon became fatal. George

William died at his beloved Wienhausen hunting lodge on 28 August 1705, having not seen his daughter for ten long years. Once the apple of his eye, he had missed his one last opportunity to bury the hatchet.

Had Sophia Dorothea had any lingering hopes of mercy and with it, freedom, they now vanished. She and her mother were left in the hands of George and he lost no time in ordering Éléonore out of the castle in Celle that had been her home for her entire married life. Éléonore took up residence in Wienhausen, where her beloved husband had died in her arms, and Celle was absorbed into Hanover, where George reigned with Melusine still at his side, his wife in everything but the law.

Éléonore made one last plea to George. She was ageing fast and the visits to Ahlden, always arduous, were now made more difficult by the increased distance from her new home. She asked whether Sophia Dorothea might be permitted to join her in the Lüneburg residence that George William had commissioned for her. George was as unswerving as ever. The answer was no.

Time was running out for those who had been players in this scandalous game. Ernest Augustus and George William were dead, whilst Figuelotte, Dowager Electress Sophia's beloved daughter, also passed away in 1705[13]. Count von Platen lived until 1709, to be replaced in his role as chief minister by the scheming Bernstorff, who was promoted to the rank of count at the same time. Yet despite all these deaths, 1705 was also a year for bittersweet news and in her Ahlden seclusion, Sophia Dorothea heard that both of her children were to marry.

Sophia Dorothea learned of this news from her mother, who told her that George Augustus was to marry Caroline of Ansbach, whilst Sophia Dorothea, still only 18, would be wed to her cousin, Frederick William of Brandenburg, son of Figuelotte, and heir to the crown of Prussia. It was she who brought Eleonore von dem Knesebeck in from the cold, appointing her as lady-in-waiting just as she had been to her own mother for so many turbulent years.

And so, it seemed, Sophia Dorothea would be forgotten. Or she would have been, if not for the naughty pen of Duke Anthony Ulrich. He used the tragic tale of her failed marriage as the basis for a story in his multi-volume work, *Die Römische Octavia*, in which a raven-haired beauty is married to a lout. When she seeks affection from a dashing and courtly lover, they both feel his brutish wrath. Of course, this version of the relationship was never more than platonic, but the wicked husband kills his wife's paramour and divorces her, despite her pure heart. The duke changed the names, but everyone knew where he had found his inspiration.

The Hardest Parting

On 8 June 1714, the Dowager Electress Sophia died in the gardens of Herrenhausen. A few weeks later, on 1 August, Queen Anne followed her to the great beyond and George, the ill-humoured Elector of Hanover, was proclaimed King of Great Britain. He left for his new realm with a retinue of over a hundred German courtiers and hangers-on, as well as Melusine and a reluctant George Augustus. By now Sophia Dorothea was a grandmother several times over[14] but, as with all news concerning her family, no official word was sent to her. Instead she relied on her ever-frailer mother to keep her in the loop. She had no wish to be a queen but no doubt it would have given her a little bit of satisfaction to know that George, never a populist chap, was making few friends in his new realm. People wondered about the truth of his former wife's circumstance and mocked Melusine, with that mockery turning to derision when she was partially blamed for the disastrous South Sea Bubble, which nearly bankrupted the kingdom.

For year after year Sophia Dorothea continued at Ahlden, buoyed only by the visits of her elderly mother, the one person who had truly stood by her from the start. Then, on 5 February 1722, Éléonore, Duchess of Celle, died. Sophia Dorothea was now very definitely alone. Éléonore was laid to rest beside her husband and the courts of Hanover and England went into mourning. For the first time, Sophia Dorothea was formally included in proceedings and Ahlden too was placed in official mourning.

It's not difficult to imagine how hard Sophia Dorothea must have taken her mother's death. By now in her mid-fifties, she had been a prisoner for nearly thirty years and through all of that time - all of her life, in fact - the only constant support and love she had known had come from Éléonore. Now that source of support and love was gone. No doubt the secret letters she received from her daughter, also named Sophia Dorothea, provided some comfort but they were no substitute for human contact and as Queen in Prussia, a visit was something that was well within the abilities of the younger woman. It was a trip she never made, despite passing Ahlden on her way to Hanover[15]. Instead her mother had to content herself with letters, little realising that in the court of Frederick William and Sophia Dorothea, scheming was afoot.

Now that Sophia Dorothea's mother and father were both dead, Frederick William, the husband of Sophia Dorothea the younger, recalled the very generous provision that George William and Éléonore had made for their imprisoned daughter in their wills. He sought legal advice to discover who would inherit Sophia Dorothea's family fortune upon her death. Would it go to George, he asked, or would it be split between her children and by extension, benefit him?

Of course, Sophia Dorothea the younger really shouldn't have been writing to her mother at all but Frederick William was willing to let that slide if his wife would only ask her about the fate of her fortune. George was a king, he pointed out, and so he hardly needed the money. All the more for her daughter, in that case. And just to sweeten the pill and get the answer he wanted, Frederick William wasn't averse to a little misdirection, letting Sophia Dorothea think that freedom might be on the cards if she decided in his favour. As soon as he learned that her fortune was to be split equally between George Augustus and Sophia Dorothea, he told his wife to discontinue her clandestine communication with her mother, satisfied with the answer. Unknown to him, the two women continued to exchange letters.

By now an exceptionally rich woman, Sophia Dorothea employed a Prussian named Count Christian de Bar to oversee her complicated finances. He had served her late father and been recommended to her by her daughter, so she was confident in his abilities. The Duchess of Ahlden, utterly unworldly after so long behind the walls of her prison, entrusted de Bar with the management of her affairs, giving him virtually free rein to do as he pleased.

With her finances in what she hoped were safe hands, Sophia Dorothea and her daughter had other matters to discuss. Chief amongst them was a double marriage plan between Frederick and Wilhelmina, Sophia Dorothea's grandchildren by her daughter, Sophia Dorothea the younger, to their cousins, Amelia and Frederick, her grandchildren by her son, George Augustus. It was a hugely ambitious scheme that would vastly extend the influence of Hanover. Sophia Dorothea the younger needed pots of cash to make the plan a reality and hoped to receive it from her mother, who had plenty of ready money and little to spend it on tucked away at Ahlden.

She was in for a shock.

The Prussian queen had long since plotted to make this double marriage happen but to her surprise, not only did her husband loathe the idea, but so did her mother. At this point, Sophia Dorothea the younger made what must have been one of the coldest announcements her mother had ever heard. She told her that if both marriages were approved and went ahead, she would do all she could to secure Sophia Dorothea's freedom but until then, she should expect to remain in her Ahlden prison. Ultimately the scheme failed, and neither of the dynastic marriages that had been dreamed of went ahead.

In a gesture of affection and perhaps apology, the Prussian queen sent her mother, 'two portraits in miniature set in gold; a gold repeater watch framed with cornelian, with chain seal and gold hook; an étui of mother-of-pearl, with side garnished in like manner; and a snuff box, covered with a rare agate'. Sophia Dorothea returned the whole lot to Berlin, with the exception of, 'the two portraits, which I shall retain'.

Still she held out hope of a reunion with her daughter and when Sophia Dorothea the younger came to Hanover in 1725, her mother dressed herself in a magnificent gown and jewels and waited to receive her.

Sophia Dorothea, Queen in Prussia, never arrived. She went straight on to Hanover, instructed by her husband not to stop in Ahlden.

It shook the duchess to her core.

Sophia Dorothea turned to Count de Bar to help her escape, ignoring her daughter's warnings that he might not be as trustworthy as they had once believed. De Bar's influence was now entirely unchecked and he used her money as though it were his own, spending frivolously with one hand whilst assuring Sophia Dorothea that he was acting only in her interests with the other. He sold off her bonds on the stock market and pocketed most of the money they made and all the time she wrote to him in passionate terms, begging him to come to Ahlden. Indeed, when you read the following lines, written by Sophia Dorothea to the count, remember that *this* nobleman was her financial adviser, not her soul mate. Yet passion was never far from the surface for the Duchess of Ahlden.

> 'Words cannot express all I think, all I have always thought without the least diminution, all I shall never cease to think. In the name of God, be always the same to me, as I shall be to you till my latest breath.'

When Sophia Dorothea eventually discovered that de Bar had been embezzling her even as she had dreamt he would be the one to secure her freedom, it was the final blow for the desperate woman. After more than three decades in captivity, kept from her children, her lover lost to her, she could stand it no more.

The Darkest Night

Behind the walls of Ahlden House, the celebrated, beautiful and vibrantly passionate young woman had become old. Her feted tresses were now white, her life one of lonely routine. She had lost all those who mattered to her and in their place was the endless round of worship, philanthropy and administration and that six mile carriage ride, day in, day out, as unchanged now as it had been thirty years earlier. Is it any wonder that a woman so lively, so filled with nervous energy, eventually couldn't sustain her spark any longer?

In late October 1726, as the nights drew in and the shadows lengthened, Sophia Dorothea retired to bed, never to walk the halls of Ahlden House again. Perhaps George heard the words of that French prophetess in his ear because from Hanover came the very best physicians, charged with preserving the life of his former spouse at any cost. For weeks they observed their patient but there was nothing that medicine could do. Sophia Dorothea's decline wasn't one that a tonic could treat.

At 11.00 pm on 13 November 1726, Sophia Dorothea, Duchess of Ahlden, died. She was 60-years-old. More than half her life had been spent as a prisoner of her husband's malice.

Post Mortem

Upon receiving news of Sophia Dorothea's death, the court of Hanover went into mourning and so too did the court of Prussia, where her daughter was queen. In England, George greeted the news by taking a trip to the theatre in the company of his mistress. Even as he applauded the performance, a stern ticking off was winging its way to Hanover and Prussia. At the latter it was ignored, and official mourning continued.

As officials from Hanover descended on Ahlden and began burning papers, the body of Sophia Dorothea was encased in a lead coffin and removed to the vault of Ahlden House, where it remained for weeks. Whilst Sophia Dorothea languished unburied, the will in which she divided her wealth between her children was burned and everything she had owned, including her inherited fortune, went into the coffers of her ex-husband.

As winter passed, the Aller broke its banks and water poured into the castle grounds, making a marshland of the gardens. Though gravediggers valiantly attempted to dig a suitable plot for the late duchess, the coffin simply refused to stay buried and eventually it was taken back to the vault, awaiting new instructions from England.

Little did they know that in St James's Palace, George wasn't taking advice from his ministers, but from the dead. As Sophia Dorothea lay in her leaden coffin, Melusine woke in the darkest hours of the night from a prophetic dream. Just as the prophetess had warned George that his own death would soon follow that of his former wife, now that former wife was paying calls on his mistress. Sophia Dorothea had visited her, Melusine told George, and she had demanded that she be buried not in Ahlden, but at Celle. If her demands were not met, she would torment George from beyond the grave to his dying day.

George didn't need to be told twice. In the spring of 1727, six months after Sophia Dorothea's death, orders were received from England to move her to the ducal burial vaults at Celle. There should be no ceremony, said the messenger, and no fanfare. The burial was to be as quiet and unobtrusive as possible. The orders were carried out by night and Sophia Dorothea was laid to rest beside her ancestors at last, her coffin unmarked but for a small plaque on which was recorded her name and dates of birth and death. Her titles weren't mentioned and for all the busts, plaques and statues that memorialise her family in the church where she rests, there was no such memorial for Sophia Dorothea. In death she was to be forgotten, just as George had hoped her to be in life.

Only now his hated wife was dead did her former husband pause for thought. He was haunted by the words of the French prophetess who warned that he should, 'take care of his wife, as he would not survive her a year,' and was determined to prove her wrong.

Needless to say, he didn't.

One deliciously dark legend states that on her deathbed, Sophia Dorothea wrote a fierce letter to George which was thrust at him through the window of his carriage during his last trip to Hanover. In it, she supposedly told him that he would stand before God and be judged within a year and a day of her death. Some said this letter was the cause of the stroke that killed him. Whether that's apocryphal or not, on 11 June 1727, during a visit to his homeland, the prophecy came true. Struck down by a massive stroke just a few days earlier, George I of Great Britain died.

One-nil to the French prophetess.

George Augustus, the son who had longed in vain to see Sophia Dorothea one last time, was now the king and one of his first acts was to return the banished portraits to the walls of the palace. Robert Walpole, that political titan, remembered that, 'the morning after the news of the death of George the First had reached London, Mrs. Howard observed (in the antechamber of the king's apartment) a picture of a woman in the electoral robes, which proved to be that of Sophia'[16]. It's possibly a fiction, as it's difficult to imagine how Sophia Dorothea would have managed to be painted in electoral robes whilst incarcerated at Ahlden, though perhaps it was a fanciful portrait that her son commissioned[17]. If so that commission and the portrait itself have long since been lost to history. Several years later he made a visit to Herrenhausen to examine Sophia Dorothea's personal papers, sure that they would confirm her innocence.

Finally the unfortunate woman's son was able to read her story in her own words. What secrets they contained, we will never know. George Augustus had always believed Sophia Dorothea was innocent of adultery and defended her name, yet the information he learned in Herrenhausen changed that forever. The contents of those papers shattered the king and he had them burned. From that day on, he never spoke of his mother again.

Afterword

'Alas! I love my destruction,
And nurse a fire within my breast
Which will speedily consume me.
I am well aware of my perdition,
Because I have aspired to love
Where I should only have worshipped.'

152

When Count Philip Christoph von Königsmarck wrote those lines to his lover, Sophia Dorothea, Electoral Princess of Hanover, they were just one stitch in a patchwork of romance, intrigue and, ultimately, catastrophe. From her spoiled girlhood in Celle to her lonely incarceration at Ahlden, her life truly ran the gamut from charmed to cursed.

Confined to her genteel prison, Sophia Dorothea was supposed to vanish like a conjurer's assistant. Yet she never quite disappeared and as the mother of George II, she played a vital role not only in the history of the United Kingdom, but of Europe. Without her the world would have been a different place and though she may have been locked away, her memory has persisted.

Today Sophia Dorothea's fate continues to fascinate as a grim fairytale that was all too real. No matter how much her husband hoped that she would be forgotten, she lives on, as vibrant today as she was more than three centuries ago when she took up her pen and wrote, 'My only pleasure is to make you remember me'.

And to this day, we do.

Appendix A

A Note on Letters

Much of what we now know about the love affair between Sophia Dorothea and Count Philip Christoph von Königsmarck can be gleaned from the letters the couple exchanged during their brief three year affair. They began innocently enough before exploding into florid passions and declarations of love, with signatures written in blood and even threats of murderous bears!

The veracity of the letters that were purportedly exchanged between Sophia Dorothea and Königsmarck has been the subject of debate for many years. Though few letters from Sophia Dorothea remain, those from her paramour are numerous. Some eventually came into the custody of Frederick the Great, who placed them in the safe keeping of the Royal Secret Archives of State in Berlin, whilst others are kept in the archive of the University Library of Lund, in Sweden.

Extracts from the letters were first published by WH Wilkins in 1900 in his book, *The Love of an Uncrowned Queen*, and few biographers can have been kinder to their subject than this august commentator. In Wilkins' immensely romanticised work, the story of George and Sophia Dorothea has all the trappings of a fairytale, complete with the Electress Sophia as a heartless mother-in-law, Clara von Platen as a wicked villainess and Sophia Dorothea as one of the most quintessential damsels in distress ever committed to print. In fiction all of this wouldn't raise too many eyebrows, but when it comes to the facts in one of the strangest marriages in royal history, the lines cannot be drawn so broadly. Instead we find ourselves faced not with good and evil, but with shades of grey. Yet it's the sheer melodrama of the letters that have caused some commentators to place them squarely in the world of the fictional. For a soldier, it must be said, Königsmarck certainly had a poetic turn of phrase.

The journey of the letters to Lund and Berlin owes much to Königsmarck's sister, Aurora. She became a vital intermediary between the lovers and many of the missives exchanged by her brother and his paramour were later entrusted to her custody. When the secret affair was made public, Eleonore von dem Knesebeck, Sophia Dorothea's confidante, swore that her mistress had always returned Königsmarck's letters to him once she had read them, as she feared that they would be discovered if she kept them in her own rooms. It would appear, therefore, that he gave them to his sister for safe keeping.

Following the disappearance of Königsmarck, Aurora entrusted the letters to another sister, Amalia von Königsmarck, the wife of Count Carl Gustav Löwenhaupt. Countess Löwenhaupt died in 1740 and amongst the papers she left to her son were the letters she had been given. They passed down the family line from one to the next until they were eventually bequeathed to the University of Lund, where they were viewed in their original French by Wilkins. Wilkins pored over the papers and picked out mentions of court life and dates, which he found corresponded perfectly to the business that was taking place in Hanover and Celle at the time. The letters, the press proclaimed, were the real deal.

> 'That the correspondence here published for the first time is authentic Mr. Wilkins unquestionably proves. The whereabouts of the letters can be traced from hand to hand up to the moment when the ink on them was still wet. Neither Königsmarck nor Sophie [sic] Dorothea ventured to keep the other's letters for long, and when a certain number had accumulated both parties confided them to Aurora Königsmarck, the Count's sufficiently notorious sister. Aurora, because of her roving and adventurous life, thought it more prudent to pass them on to the safe keeping of the one respectable member of the Königsmarck family, the Countess Lewenhaupt [sic]. who had married a Swedish noble and was settled in Sweden. This lady, on her death-bed, gave them to her son, telling him to cherish them with great care, as they had cost "her brother his life, and a King's mother her freedom."'[1]

It sounds like quite a story in itself!

155

The letters that were to be found in Berlin had enjoyed an equally adventurous history before they finally arrived in the archive, having first surfaced in the hands of Queen Louisa Ulrika of Sweden, Sophia Dorothea's granddaughter, in 1754. It was she who gave them to her brother, Frederick the Great, who kept them until his death. Their next stop was the archives in Berlin.

Whilst some of the letters are in Sophia Dorothea's handwriting, and some in that of Eleonore von dem Knesebeck, her amanuensis, those that came from the count were all written personally. In his messy handwriting and imperfect French Königsmarck poured out his heart, a hardened soldier and florid poet in one. And he couldn't have hoped for a more willing recipient than Sophia Dorothea. At times the two seemed to be competing to write the purplest prose. They had fallen in love and by God, they were going to be as dramatic as possible in expressing it!

Mindful of discovery, the couple employed an elaborate code to avoid detection, giving the players in the story both pseudonyms and identifying numbers. It is as though a childish game has spilled over into adulthood. The code names were rather telling too, and in some cases far from flattering.

> Léonisse/La Couer Gauche/La Petite Louche: Sophia Dorothea
> Le Chevalier/Tercis: Königsmarck
> Le Reformeur: George Louis
> Don Diego: Ernest Augustus
> La Romaine: Sophia
> La Perspective: Clara von Platen
> Le Grandeur: George William
> La Pedagogue: Éléonore Desmier d'Olbreuse
> La Confidente/La Sentinelle/La Gouvernante: Eleonore von dem Knesebeck
> L'Aventuriere: Aurora Königsmarck

The code names extend still further to include the brothers of George, a few Hanoverian ministers and more. The couple also employed a numerical code in which each player was assigned a number, with male names beginning 1 and female 2, whilst locations were given a number that begins in 3.

100: Ernest Augustus
101: George William
102: George Louis
120: Königsmarck

200: Sophia
201: Sophia Dorothea
202: Clara von Platen
207: Melusine von der Schulenburg
214: Eleonore von dem Knesebeck
227: Éléonore Desmier d'Olbreuse

300: Hanover
302: Herrenhausen
305: Celle

It was a cypher that foxed at least one biographer. Professor WF Palmblad of the University of Upsala reproduced the letters in his 1847 book, *Briefwechsel des Grafen Königsmark and der Prinzessin Sophie Dorothea von Celle*, but he found himself swiftly tangled in the numerical cypher, not to mention the confusing chronology of the often undated letters. The subsequent inaccuracies that arose from this misunderstanding led some to speculate that the letters couldn't be genuine, but Wilkins' painstaking work to establish the chronology and compare court affairs mentioned against the dispatches of British envoy Sir William Dutton Colt did much to establish the veracity of the correspondence. His efforts were later further improved upon by historian Georg Schnath, who succeeded in the monumental task of dating all of the existing letters from the first to the last.

If the letters were forgeries they were masterful. More likely they were genuine and we should consider them as such when we delve into the murky world of Hanoverian court politics.

Letters, as we have learned, could be fatal.

Appendix B

The Agreement

The full text of the agreement signed on 15 May 1676 at Celle by Ernest Augustus and George William regarding the legitimisation of Sophia Dorothea and his marriage to Éléonore is as follows.

1. The Bishop [Ernest Augustus] promises not to oppose the said marriage, but will acknowledge and countenance the said Countess [Éléonore], and the children that may be born of this marriage; and also the daughter now living, Sophia Dorothea, agreeing to uphold her in the possession of her estates, and in her state and rank conferred upon her, and which may be conferred upon her, by the Emperor, and his Serene Highness Duke George William, in so far as such may not be to the prejudice of the heirs of the Bishop, as regards the sovereignty of this Duchy and its appurtenances.
2. The heirs of the Bishop are bound to respect the Duke's settlement on the Countess and her heirs.
3. The Duke promises that this marriage shall not be to the disadvantage of the Bishop or his male heirs, on the Duke's death; and his claim of succession as secured by the Duke's written and verbal promises, and the sanction of the Emperor, is confirmed.
4. Should one or more children be born in this marriage, they are to remain satisfied with the property the Duke, with the consent of the Bishop, may leave them at his decease and renounce any pretension to the Duchy and its appurtenances, as long as male heirs exist in the Bishop's family.
5. Neither sons nor daughters born in this marriage can be permitted to make use of the Ducal coat of arms; but, should Sophia Dorothea marry a prince of ancient family, she will be allowed to use the title and coat of arms of a princess by birth of Brunswick-Lüneburg.

The Agreement

6. The oath of allegiance of the inhabitants of the Duchy of Lüneburg and its appurtenances, as also that of the civil and military authorities, are to undergo alteration, and the deputies of the country are not to be bound by their oath of allegiance, as far as regards the posterity of Duke George William, respecting which they will be informed by him.

7. The Duke renounces in the strongest manner all advantages likely to accrue to himself and his children; and if the pretensions of the Bishop and his heirs to the Duchy be called by them in question in any way, such are declared to be contrary to the intention of this agreement.

8. In further confirmation, and to avoid difficulties, the Duke and the Bishop will implore the Emperor to ratify this contract of marriage, and to append to it the necessary clauses, particularly that his Imperial Majesty and all his posterity do not allow anything to be done against it, that it be enrolled in the imperial courts, and that any one acting in opposition to it incur a penalty of a thousand marks.

9. On obtaining the imperial sanction, the Duke will alter in council the feudal oaths of allegiance, to the manner in which they are to be henceforth administered.

10. All privy counsellors, and servants of the government and its domains, all generals, colonels, captains, and commanders, are to ratify this change under their hands and seals. As regards the military, the Duke furthermore promises that, after they have entered their quarters, and when they have been mustered, which will quickly follow, they shall take the oath in the altered form.

11. Before this marriage is consummated, the Duke will summon before him the deputies of the country, in the customary manner, and acquaint them with this arrangement, and obtain from them an oath to respect the claims of the Bishop and his descendants; two copies of their agreement to this is to be made, one for the Duke and the other for the Bishop.

12. Should the lady be further blessed with offspring, the Duke agrees to publish to all his subjects, that, after his death the succession must rest with the Bishop, and descend from him, from father to son, according to an arrangement made when the Duke first entered upon the government, as his own offspring will be otherwise provided for at his decease.

In the foregoing stipulation, a great deal is stated respecting the Duke's anxious desire for the peace and welfare of his people having led him to enter into this arrangement, and his hope that after his decease they will be faithful and obedient to the successor whom he has appointed them.

13. The Duke will settle with the Bishop the feudal rights and usages, and have the nobility and magistrates personally informed of this succession, and forward information to the towns and domains.

Lastly, the Duke will write to his brother Duke John Frederick, and to his cousin Duke Rudolph Augustus, the necessary information for the benefit of their princely family, with a request that, for the preservation of peace and the good of the country, this agreement may be respected.

Bibliography

Agnew, David CA. *Protestant Exiles from France in the Reign of Louis XIV: Vol I.* London: Reeves & Turner, 1871.

Alexander, Marc. *Royal Murder.* UK: Willow Books, 2012.

Anonymous. *Cottage Hearth, Vol 12-13.* Boston: Milliken and Spencer, 1886.

Anonymous. *The Georgian Era, Vol I.* London: Vizetelly, Branston and Co, 1832.

Anonymous. *The Life of the Princess of Zell, Wife of George I King of England.* London: Privately published, undated.

Anonymous. *Memorials Of Affairs of State In The Reigns of Q. Elizabeth and K. James I, Vol III.* London: T Ward, 1725.

Anonymous (ed.). *University Library of Autobiography: Vol V.* New York, F Tyler Daniels, 1918.

Basset, Thomas. *The Tryal and Condemnation of George Borosky alias Boratzi, Christopher Vratz, and John Stern; for the Barbarous Murder of Thomas Thynn, Esq.* London: Thomas Basset, 1682.

Beatty, Michael A. *The English Royal Family of America, from Jamestown to the American Revolution.* Jefferson: McFarland & Co, 2003.

Beauclaire, Horric de. *A Mésalliance in the House of Brunswick.* London: Remington & Co, 1886.

Belsham, William. *History of Great Britain from the Revolution to the Accession of the House of Hanover, Vol II.* London: GG & J Robinson, 1793.

Belsham, William. *Memoirs of the Kings of Great Britain of the House of Brunswic-Luneburg, Vol I.* London: C Dilly, 1798.

Black, Jeremy. *The Hanoverians: The History of a Dynasty.* London: Hambledon and London, 2007.

Brown, John. *Anecdotes and Characters of the House of Brunswick.* London: T and J Allman, 1821.

Brown, John (ed.). *The Historical Galleries of Criminal Portraitures, Foreign and Domestic: Vol II.* Manchester: J Gleave, 1823.

Campbell Orr, Clarissa. *Queenship in Europe 1660–1815: The Role of the Consort*. Cambridge: Cambridge University Press, 2004.

Carlyle, Thomas. *Fraser's Magazine for Town and Country. Vol XLVIII*. London: John W Parker and Son, 1853.

Chapman, Hester W. *Privileged Persons*. London: Reynal & Hitchcock, 1966.

Clarke. *The Georgian Era: Volume I*. London, Vizetelly: Branston and Co., 1832.

Clarke, John, Godwin Ridley, Jasper and Fraser, Antonia. *The Houses of Hanover & Saxe-Coburg-Gotha*. Berkeley: University of California Press, 2000.

Coxe, William. M*emoirs of the Life and Administration of Sir Robert Walpole, Earl of Orford, Vol I*. London: T Cadell, Jun. and W Davies, 1798.

Coxe, William. M*emoirs of the Life and Administration of Sir Robert Walpole, Earl of Orford, Vol 1*. London: Longman, Hurst, Rees, Orme, and Brown, 1816.

Coxe, William. *Memoirs of the Life and Administration of Sir Robert Walpole, Earl of Orford, Vol II*. London: T Cadell, Jun and W Davies, 1798.

Crompton, Louis. *Homosexuality and Civilization*. London: The Belknap Press, 2003.

Curzon, Catherine. *Kings of Georgian Britain*. Barnsley: Pen and Sword Books Ltd, 2017.

Curzon, Catherine. *Queens of Georgian Britain*. Barnsley: Pen and Sword Books Ltd, 2017.

Curzon, Catherine. *Sophia: Mother of Kings*. Barnsley: Pen and Sword Books Ltd, 2019.

D'Auvergne, Edward. *The History of the Campagne in Flanders, For the Year 1697*. London: John Newton, 1698.

Doran, John. *Lives of the Queens of England of the House of Hanover, Volume I*. London: Richard Bentley & Son, 1875.

Draper, Sarah. *Memoirs of the Princess of Zell: Vol I*. London: William Lane, 1796.

Duggan, JN. *Sophia of Hanover: From Winter Princess to Heiress of Great Britain, 1630 - 1714*. London: Peter Owen, 2013.

Evelyn, John. *The Diary of John Evelyn, Vol III*. New York: The Macmillan Company, 1906.

Evelyn, John. *Memoirs Illustrative of the Life and Writings of John Evelyn, Esq FRS, Vol II*. London: Henry Colburn, 1819.

Bibliography

Fisher, George. *A Companion and Key to the History of England.* London: Simpkin and Marshall, 1832.

Forester, H (trans.). *Memoirs of Sophia, Electress of Hanover, 1630-1680.* London: T Bentley & Son, 1888.

Gold, Claudia. *The King's Mistress.* London: Quercus, 2012.

Gothein, Marie Luise Schroeter and Wright, Walter P. *A History of Garden Art.* Cambridge: Cambridge University Press, 2014.

Greenwald, Helen M (ed.). *The Oxford Handbook of Opera.* Oxford: Oxford University Press, 2014.

Gregg, Edward. *Queen Anne.* New York: Yale University Press, 2014.

Hall, Matthew. *The Royal Princesses of England.* London: George Routledge and Sons, 1871.

Halliday, Andrew. *A General History of the House of Guelph.* London: Thomas and George Underwood, 1821.

Hatton, Ragnhild. *George I.* London: Thames and Hudson, 1978.

Henderson, Ernest F. *The Present Status of the Königsmark Question.* The American Historical Review, 1898.

Henderson, Ernest F. *Side Lights on English History.* New York: Henry Holt and Company, 1900.

Herman, Eleanor. *Sex with the Queen.* London: Harper Collins, 2009.

Hunt, Margaret. *Women in Eighteenth-Century Europe.* New York: Routledge, 2010.

Hunt, Violet. *The Desirable Alien at Home in Germany.* London: Chatto and Windus, 1913.

Imbert, Hugues. *Histoire de Thouars.* Niort: L. Clouzot, 1871.

Jordan, Ruth. *Sophia Dorothea.* New York: George Braziller, 1972.

Kemble, John M. *State Papers and Correspondence Illustrative of the Social and Political State of Europe.* London: John W Parker and Son, 1857.

Kroll, Maria. *Sophie, Electress of Hanover.* London: Victor Gollancz, 1973.

McCalman, Archibald Hamilton. *An Abridged History of England.* New York: Trow's Printing and Bookbinding Company, 1880.

Macaulay, Thomas Babington. *The History of England from the Accession of James II, Vol IV.* New York: Harper & Brothers, 1856.

Mangan, JJ. *The King's Favour.* New York: St Martin's Press, 1991.

Melville, Lewis. *The First George in Hanover and England, Vol I.* London: Sir Isaac Pitman and Sons, Ltd, 1908.

Molloy, J Fitzgerald. *Court Life Below Stairs of London Under the First Georges, Vol I.* London: Hurst and Blackett, 1882.

Morand, Paul. *The Captive Princess: Sophia Dorothea of Celle*. Florida: American Heritage Press, 1972.

Neigebaur, JF. *Eleonore d'Olbreuse, die Stammutter der Königshäuser von England, Hannover und Preußen*. Brunswick: Eduard Leibrod, 1859.

Noble, Mark. *A History of the College of Arms and the Lives of all the Kings, Heralds, and Pursuivants, from the Reign of Richard III*. London: J Debrett, 1804.

Pearce, Edward. *The Great Man: Sir Robert Walpole: Scoundrel, Genius and Britain's First Prime Minister*. London: Random House, 2011.

Ranke, Leopold von. *A History of England Principally in the Seventeenth Century: Volume V*. Oxford: The Clarendon Press, 1875.

Reresby, Sir John. *Memoirs of Sir John Reresby of Thrybergh, Bart, MP for York*. London: Longmans, Green, and Co., 1875.

Sanderson, Edgar. *History of England and the British Empire*. London: Frederick Warne and Co, 1893.

Saussure, Cesar de. *A Foreign View of England in the Reigns of George I & George II*. London: John Murray, 1902.

Shawe-Taylor, Desmond and Burchard, Wolf. *The First Georgians: Art and Monarchy 1714–1760*. London: Royal Collection Trust, 2014.

Sinclair-Stevenson, Christopher. *Blood Royal: The Illustrious House of Hanover*. London: Faber & Faber, 2012.

Smith, Alex. *A Compleat History of the Lives and Robberies of the most Notorious Highway-Men, Foot-Pads, Shop-Lifts, and Cheats, Vol II*. London: Sam. Briscoe, 1719.

Smucker, Samuel M. *A History of the Four Georges, Kings of England*. New York: D Appleton and Company, 1860.

Somerset, Anne. *Ladies-in-Waiting: From The Tudors to the Present Day*. London: Castle Book, 2004.

Strickland, Agnes and Strickland, Elizabeth. *Lives of the Queens of Scotland and English Princesses, Vol VIII*. London: William Blackwood and Sons, 1859.

Strickland, Agnes. *Queens of England, Vol III*. Boston: Estes & Lauriat, 1894.

Thackeray, William Makepeace. *The Four Georges*. London: Smith, Elder, & Co, 1862.

Thackeray, William Makepeace. *The Works of William Makepeace Thackeray: Vol XIX*. London: Smith, Elder, & Co, 1869.

Thurloe, John. *A Collection of the State Papers of John Thurloe, Vol II.* London: The Executor of the late Mr Fletcher Gyles, 1741.

Tytler, Sarah. *Six Royal Ladies of the House of Hanover.* London: Hutchinson & Co., 1898.

Wahrman, Dror. *Mr. Collier's Letter Racks.* Oxford: Oxford University Press, 2012.

Walpole, Horace. *Complete Works of Horace Walpole.* Hastings: Delphi Classics, 2015.

Walpole, Horace and Cunningham, Peter (ed.). *The Letters of Horace Walpole, Earl of Orford: Vol I.* London: Bickers and Son, 1877.

Walpole, Horace and Wright, John. *The Letters of Horace Walpole: Vol I, 1735-1748.* Philadelphia: Lea and Blanchard, 1842.

Ward, Adolphus William. *The Electress Sophia and the Hanoverian Succession.* London: Longmans. Green and Co, 1909.

Ward, Adolphus William. *Great Britain and Hanover: Some Aspects of the Personal Union.* Oxford: The Clarendon Press, 1899.

Ward, Sean (trans). *Memoirs (1630-1680).* Toronto: Centre for Reformation and Renaissance Studies and ITER, 2014.

Wilkins, William Henry. *The Love of an Uncrowned Queen.* London: Hutchinson & Co, 1900.

Williams, H Noel. *The Love Affairs of the Condés.* London: Methuen & Co, Ltd, 1912.

Williams, Robert Folkestone. *Memoirs of Sophia Dorothea, Consort of George I, Vol I.* London: Henry Colburn, 1845.

Williams, Robert Folkestone. *Memoirs of Sophia Dorothea, Consort of George I, Vol II.* London: Henry Colburn, 1845.

Wraxall, N William. *Memoirs of the Courts of Berlin, Dresden, Warsaw and Vienna, Vol I.* London: A Strahan, 1800.

Newspapers

All newspaper clippings are reproduced © The British Library Board; in addition to those cited, innumerable newspapers were consulted.

The Leicester Chronicle: or, Commercial and Agricultural Advertiser (Leicester, England), Saturday, 13 October, 1855.

London Gazette (London, England), 29 July,1689 - 1 August,1689; Issue 2475.

London Mercury or Moderate Intelligencer (London, England), 11 February, 1689 – 14 February, 1689.

The Morning Post (London, England), Thursday, 10 May, 1900; Issue 39916.

Post Man and the Historical Account (London, England), 30 July, 1700 – 1 August, 1700; Issue 784.

Present State of Europe or the Historical and Political Mercury (London, England), Tuesday, 1 November, 1692; Issue 10.

The Times (London, England), Tuesday, 30 December, 1890; Issue 33208.

Websites Consulted

British History Online (http://www.british-history.ac.uk)

British Newspapers 1600–1950 (http://gdc.gale.com/products/19th-centurybritish-library-newspapers-part-i-and-part-ii/)

Georgian Papers Online (https://gpp.royalcollection.org.uk)

Hansard (http://hansard.millbanksystems.com/index.html)

Historical Texts (http://historicaltexts.jisc.ac.uk)

House of Commons Parliamentary Papers (http://parlipapers.chadwyck.co.uk/marketing/index.jsp)

JSTOR (www.jstor.org)

The National Archives (http://www.nationalarchives.gov.uk)

Oxford Dictionary of National Biography (http://www.oxforddnb.com)

State Papers Online (https://www.gale.com/intl/primary-sources/state-papers-online)

The Times Digital Archive (http://gale.cengage.co.uk/times-digital-archive/times-digital-archive-17852006.aspx)

Endnotes

Introduction

1   Coxe, William (1816). *Memoirs of the Life and Administration of Sir Robert Walpole, Earl of Orford, Vol 1*. London: Longman, Hurst, Rees, Orme, and Brown, p.260.

Act One: Bride

1   *The Leicester Chronicle: or, Commercial and Agricultural Advertiser* (Leicester, England), Saturday, 13 October, 1855.

2   The couple had already lost their eldest son, Henry Frederick, who drowned in 1629 at the age of 15. It was a death from which his father never truly recovered.

3   Charles II, then Prince of Wales, was in Heidelberg seeking support in his battle against Parliament. He and Sophia were cousins and Elizabeth hoped a marriage between them would both take her daughter off her hands and see her secure an excellent match. However, when Sophia correctly guessed that Charles was more interested in using her to network with her rich friends than he was in her good looks and charm, she decided there and then that they would never be married.

4   Ward, Sean (trans.) (2014). *Memoirs (1630-1680)*. Toronto: Centre for Reformation and Renaissance Studies and ITER.

5   Ibid.

6   The Renunciation of Marriage agreement signed by the brothers reads as follows: 'Having perceived the urgent necessity of taking into consideration how our House of this line may best be provided with heirs and be perpetuated in the future, yet having been and remaining up to the present date both unable and unwilling in my own person to engage in any marriage contract, I have rather induced my brother, Ernest Augustus, to declare that, on condition

of receiving from me a renunciation of marriage for myself, written and signed with my own hand, in favour of himself and his heirs male, he is prepared forthwith and without delay to enter into holy matrimony, and, as may be hoped, soon to bestow the blessing of heirs on people and country, as has been agreed and settled between him and myself; and where whereas my brother, Ernest Augustus, for reasons before mentioned, has entered into a marriage contract with her Highness Princess Sophia, which contract he purposes shortly to fulfil, so I, on my side, not only on account of my word given to and pledged, but also of my own free will and consent, desire to ratify and confirm the aforesaid conditions to my before mentioned brother, and promise, so long as the said Princess and my brother continue in life and in the bonds of matrimony, or after their decease leave heirs male, that I neither will nor shall on any account enter into, much less carry out, any marriage on tract with any person, and with nothing else than to spend what remains to me of life entirely *in celibatu*, to the extent that the heirs male of the before-mentioned Princess and of my brother, in whose favour this renunciation is made, may attain and succeed to the sovereignty over one or both of these our principalities. For the safer and truer assurance of all which conditions I have, with my own hand, written and signed this renunciation and sealed it with my seal, and thereafter handed it over with all due care to my brother's own charge and keeping. So done at Hanover.'

7   Ward, Sean (trans.) (2014). *Memoirs (1630-1680)*. Toronto: Centre for Reformation and Renaissance Studies and ITER.
8   Sophia miscarried twins in 1664. Two years later she gave birth to twin sons. One of the twins was stillborn whilst the other survived.
9   The duchess was married to Henry de La Trémoille, Duke of Thouars. Their son, Henri Charles, made an excellent dynastic marriage to Emilie of Hesse-Kassel, daughter of William V, Landgrave of Hesse-Kassel.
10 Breda is forever associated with Charles II thanks to the *Declaration of Breda*. This 1660 document laid out Charles' conditions for accepting the English crown and thereby restoring the monarchy in England.
11 Christian Louis passed away on 15 March 1665, forcing George William to return to his homeland. Here he found that John Frederick

had seized control of wealthy Celle, in direct contradiction to the wishes of their late father. George William and Ernest Augustus joined forces against him to demand that the territories be properly divided and only when they stood on the brink of civil war was an agreement reached. John Frederick surrendered Celle to George William and the remaining lands were distributed between all three living brothers.

12 By now appointed Bishop of Osnabrück, Ernest Augustus and Sophia made their home in the Bishop's Palace at Iburg.

13 Liselotte was the pet name of Elizabeth Charlotte, Madame Palatine, the daughter of Sophia's brother, Charles I Louis, Elector Palatine. She spent several years in her childhood living with Ernest Augustus and Sophia and later remembered them as the happiest of her life. Sophia and Liselotte remained as close as mother and daughter and Liselotte eventually married the flamboyantly homosexual Philippe I, Duke of Orléans, son of Louis XIII. Together the couple became known as *Monsieur et Madame*.

14 Wilkins, WH (1900). *The Love of an Uncrowned Queen*. London: Hutchinson & Co, p.25.

15 In 1685, Rudolph Augustus officially appointed his brother co-regent. When Rudolph Augustus died in 1704, Anthony Ulrich continued to rule alone.

16 Wilkins, WH (1900). *The Love of an Uncrowned Queen*. London: Hutchinson & Co, p.31.

17 George Christopher von Hammerstein was the son of Hanover's High Bailiff and one of the court's most trusted retainers.

18 See Appendix B for the full text.

19 Williams, Robert Folkestone (1845). *Memoirs of Sophia Dorothea, Consort of George I*, Vol I. London: Henry Colburn, p.207.

20 Later ennobled as a baron and count.

21 He was just 21-years-old at the time of his death.

22 Smith, Alex (1719). *A Compleat History of the Lives and Robberies of the most Notorious Highway-Men, Foot-Pads, Shop-Lifts, and Cheats, Vol II*. London: Sam. Briscoe, p.110.

23 Sir John Reresby, 2nd Baronet, was a Member of Parliament and diarist.

24 Reresby, Sir John (1875). *Memoirs of Sir John Reresby of Thrybergh, Bart., MP for York*. London: Longmans, Green, and Co., p.240.

25 Ibid, p.241.
26 Evelyn, John (1906). *The Diary of John Evelyn, Vol III*. New York: The Macmillan Company, p.81.
27 Reresby, Sir John (1875). *Memoirs of Sir John Reresby of Thrybergh, Bart., MP for York*. London: Longmans, Green, and Co., p.243.
28 Evelyn, John (1906). *The Diary of John Evelyn, Vol III*. New York: The Macmillan Company, p.81.
29 '24th [March]. I went to see the corpse of that obstinate creature, Colonel Vratz, the King permitting that his body should be transported to his own country, he being of a good family, and one of the first embalmed by a particular art, invented by one William Russell, a coffin-maker, which preserved the body without disbowelling [sic], or to appearance using any bituminous matter. The flesh was florid, soft, and full, as if the person were only sleeping. He had now been dead near fifteen days, and lay exposed in a very rich coffin lined with lead, too magnificent for so daring and horrid a murderer.' Evelyn, John (1906). *The Diary of John Evelyn, Vol III*. New York: The Macmillan Company, p.81.
30 Elizabeth Seymour, Duchess of Somerset, died in 1722 at the age of 55.
31 Draper, Sarah (1796). *Memoirs of the Princess of Zell: Vol I*. London: William Lane, p.19.
32 Wilkins, WH (1900). *The Love of an Uncrowned Queen*. London: Hutchinson & Co, p.54.
33 Ibid.
34 Though slightly lower on the list of royal rankings than emperor or king, elector carried a heck of a cache of its own. Since the thirteenth century, the Prince-Electors of the Holy Roman Empire were the only men allowed to vote for the next Holy Roman Emperor, and having one's duchy elevated to an electorate was a great honour.
35 That same Anne would later rule as Queen Anne between 1702 and 1714. Her marriage to Prince George of Denmark, once mooted as a suitor for Sophia Dorothea, left no living heir despite more than a dozen pregnancies. That lack of an heir set the stage for the dawn of the Georgian era.
36 In 1689 Ernest Augustus built an opera house at the Leineschloss, where he held enormous and glamorous entertainment extravaganzas.
37 Royal MSS, vol clx, folio 230.

38 Anonymous (1886). *Cottage Hearth, Vol 12-13*. Boston: Milliken and Spencer, p.284.

39 Ibid.

40 Lassay lived into his eighties. Not long before he died in 1738 he published his scandalous and somewhat fanciful memoirs and letters. Included among them was the letter he claimed to have written to Sophia Dorothea imploring her to end their affair rather than risk her reputation. Though he proclaimed that he would die without her company, he managed to outlive virtually everyone in this tale! The fanciful and eccentric Lassay married three times. Following his death, he was buried alongside his trio of late wives in the Benedictine Convent at Lassay-les-Châteaux.

41 Doran, John (1875). *Lives of the Queens of England of the House of Hanover, Volume I*. London: Richard Bentley & Son, p.36.

42 Sophia Dorothea of Hanover married her cousin, Frederick William I of Prussia, in 1706. Amongst their fourteen children was a little boy who went on to achieve legendary royal status as Frederick the Great. Sophia Dorothea lived on until 1757, making her one of the few players in this tale to outlive the saucy Marquis de Lassay!

43 Countess Elizabeth Báthory has become notorious for her supposed love of bathing in or even drinking the blood of virgins. Born in 1560, this Hungarian noblewoman is believed to have been responsible for countless acts of murder and torture and was eventually arrested and imprisoned for her crimes. After the countess died in 1614, stories began to spring up alleging that she drank and bathed in the blood of her victims. They have passed into vampiric folklore but have no basis in recorded or reliable fact. Likewise, the official number of her victims stands at eighty, but a witness at the time claimed that the countess had kept a list of all her victims and believed that it numbered over 650. This list and the diary that contained it have never been recovered.

44 Sadly on this occasion it wasn't ass's milk. We shall leave that to the Daughter of the Nile!

45 Some sources have recorded her name as *Use*.

46 Sophia Charlotte of Hanover married Frederick of Hohenzollern on 8 October 1684. In 1688 they became the Elector and Electress of Brandenburg and thirteen years later, Prussian's first ever king and queen.

47 Caroline and George Augustus married in 1705.
48 Charles Talbot later became 1st Duke of Shrewsbury, William Cavendish became 1st Duke of Devonshire and Thomas Osborne became 1st Duke of Leeds. Richard Lumley was awarded the title of 1st Earl of Scarborough whilst Edward Russell and Henry Sydney became 1st Earl of Orford and 1st Earl of Romney respectively.
49 *London Mercury or Moderate Intelligencer* (London, England), February 11, 1689 - February 14, 1689.
50 Anne suffered a series of stillbirths and miscarriages between 1687 and 1688. In 1687 her two surviving children died within days of each other, neither having survived infancy. She suffered eight further stillbirths and miscarriages before her death. In addition, Anne gave birth to three surviving children but two of these died within twenty four hours of their delivery. Prince William, Duke of Gloucester, was Anne's longest-lived child and died a week after his eleventh birthday.
51 *London Gazette* (London, England), July 29, 1689 - August 1, 1689; Issue 2475.
52 The Grand Alliance was formed in 1686 as the League of Augsburg, with the intention of opposing Louis XIV's aggressive expansionism. Its membership was not consistent but it included Austria, Bavaria, Brandenburg, the Dutch Republic, Ireland, Portugal, the Rhine Palatinate, Savoy, Saxony, Spain and Sweden. When England and Scotland joined in 1689, it became known as the *Grand Alliance*.
53 *Colt's Despatch*, Hanover, 26 July, 1689.
54 *Colt's Despatch*, Hanover, 30 July, 1689.

Act Two: Lover

1 Ward, Adolphus William (1090). *The Electress Sophia and the Hanoverian Succession*. London: Longmans, Green and Co, p.503.
2 Sophia Charlotte married George's faithful servant and friend, Johann Adolf, Baron von Kielmansegg, in 1701. In recognition of her loyalty and friendship, George later bestowed the title of Countess of Darlington upon Sophia Charlotte.
3 *Colt's Despatch,* Locknam, 10 June, 1691.
4 Melusine never married, though rumours persisted that she and George underwent a clandestine marriage. She was rewarded for

her fidelity in 1719 when she was created Duchess of Kendal and remained George's constant companion until his death.

5 Sophia knew a thing or two about the power of mistresses, having watched her often manic sister-in-law lose her position to her husband's younger, less violently inclined mistress years earlier. Charlotte, the Electress Palatine, had attempted to resist her rival's encroaching influence and the result had been a divorce. Such a scandal in Hanover was unthinkable, and Sophia always accepted her own husband's mistresses with pragmatism. She would have expected Sophia Dorothea to do likewise.

6 Coxe, William (1798). *Memoirs of the Life and Administration of Sir Robert Walpole, Earl of Orford, Vol II*. London: T Cadell, Jun and W Davies, p.304.

7 John George III, Elector of Saxony, was married to Princess Anne Sophie of Denmark. During the marriage he fathered a child with his opera singing mistress, Margarita Salicola.

8 Anonymous. *The Georgian Era, Vol I* (1832). London: Vizetelly, Branston and Co, p.19.

9 The South Sea Bubble has become synonymous with ruin and bankruptcy and big business running rampantly out of control. The South Sea Company offered to buy up the national debt of Great Britain during the War of the Spanish Succession in return for a monopoly on South American trade routes once the war was concluded, in addition to five per cent interest on the repayment of the debt. Melusine played a vital role in convincing George to back the scheme and he even became a governor of the company.

   The value of shares in the South Sea Company rose to ten times their initial value yet the company directors knew that they could never hope to repay their multitude of investors. The stocks plummeted, ruining people of every social class and leading to an outcry against the king and his mistress. The fallout, both personal and national, was enormous and George's reputation took a resounding body blow as the country reeled from its near total financial collapse.

10 'William and Mary: February 1690', in *Calendar of State Papers Domestic: William and Mary, 1689-90*, ed. William John Hardy (London, 1895), pp. 441-486. British History Online http://www.british-history.ac.uk/cal-state-papers/domestic/will-mary/1689-90/pp441-486.

11 Ibid.

12 Macaulay, Thomas Babington. *The History of England from the Accession of James II, Vol IV* (1856). New York: Harper & Brothers, pp.3-4.

13 Ibid, p.5.

14 Maria Christina Königsmarck died on 17 September 1691.

15 The friend in question was Prince Christian Henry, George's brother. In the event he didn't go to the Morea after all and managed to live for a dozen more years, eventually dying in 1703 when he drowned in the Danube whilst fighting against the French at Ulm.

16 *Colt's Despatch*, Celle, 8 December, 1691.

17 The children were Anna Louise Sophie von der Schulenburg (1692-1773), Petronilla Melusina von der Schulenburg (1693-1778) and Margarethe Gertrud von Oeynhausen (1701-1726). The first two children were christened as daughters of Melusine's half-brother, Friedrich Achaz von der Schulenburg, and his wife, Margarathe Gertrud. The third child was christened as the daughter of Melusine's brother-in-law, Rabe Christoph von Oeynhausen, and his wife, Sophie Juliane. As far as the world was concerned the children were Melusine's nieces, but of course the gossips at court knew better.

18 *La Gazelle* is most likely Amalia von Königsmarck, Königsmarck's sister and the wife of Count Carl Gustav Löwenhaupt. Countess Löwenhaupt earned her codename *Gazelle* thanks to her large eyes.

19 Field-Marshal Heinrich von Podewils was born in 1615 and he was a close friend of Königsmarck. Though he had made his name and reputation fighting for the French, he was a Huguenot and left the French army to pledge his allegiance to Hanover, where he became Commander-in-Chief. He died in 1696.

20 François Henri de Montmorency-Bouteville, Duke of Piney-Luxembourg, was born in 1628 and had enjoyed a long and glittering military career. Uncompromising and fiercely loyal to the point of fanatical, he was at the head of the French army in the Spanish Netherlands from 1690 and became something of a thorn in the Grand Alliance's side. When William III supposedly complained that, 'I never can beat that cursed humpback,' Luxembourg replied, 'How does he know I have a hump? He has never seen my back.' He died in 1695.

21 Ferdinand Willem, Duke of Württemberg-Neuenstadt, later inherited the position of commander of the Garde te Voet from Count Solms when the latter was killed at the Battle of Neerwinden in 1693.

22 George almost lost his life at Neerwinden too and his unfortunate horse was shot out from beneath him!

23 In 1701 Frederick and Sophia Charlotte became the first King and Queen in Prussia.

24 *Present State of Europe or the Historical and Political Mercury* (London, England), Tuesday, November 1, 1692; Issue 10.

25 Hanover's conversion into an electorate wasn't formally completed until 1708, long after Ernest Augustus' death.

26 The highly respected Count Bielke was Sweden's ambassador to France and eventually became the governor of Swedish Pomerania.

27 Horace Walpole, that inveterate and irresistible purveyor of eighteenth century gossip, remembered the *Elephant* and the *Maypole* vividly in his letters and wrote:

'Lady Darlington, whom I saw at my mother's in my infancy, and whom I remember by being terrified at her enormous figure, was as corpulent and ample as the Duchess [Melusine] was long and emaciated. Two fierce black eyes, large and rolling beneath two lofty arched eyebrows, two acres of cheeks spread with crimson, an ocean of neck that overflowed and was not distinguished from the lower part of her body, and no part restrained by stays.'

Walpole, Horace and Cunningham, Peter (ed.) (1877). *The Letters of Horace Walpole, Earl of Orford: Vol I*. London: Bickers and Son, p.105.

28 John George IV has ties to another Georgian king as the stepfather of Caroline of Ansbach, future wife of Sophia Dorothea's own son, George II. Caroline's mother, Princess Eleonore Erdmuthe of Saxe-Eisenach, was left a widow with two young children after smallpox claimed the life of her husband, John Frederick, Margrave of Brandenburg-Ansbach. Impoverished, she agreed to marry John George IV in 1692.

The marriage was deeply unhappy and John George openly ignored his wife whilst treating his mistress, Magdalena Sibylla von Neidschütz, known as *Billa*, as his electress. John George was a violent man and Eleonore fled her husband after he threatened her with a knife. He remained at Billa's side when she contracted smallpox and the couple died within a month of each other, both succumbing to the disease.

29 Augustus later became known as *Augustus the Strong* due to his eye-opening feats of strength. In 1697, he became King of Poland, a position he held twice.

30 Among Augustus' many mistresses was Königsmarck's sister, Aurora, the woman who was entrusted with the care of so many of the lovers' letters. By the time of his death in 1733, Augustus had supposedly fathered over 350 children with his dozens of mistresses, but only one by his understandably estranged wife, Christiane Eberhardine of Brandenburg-Bayreuth. Like our own George IV, though, for all his vulgar behaviour when it came to women, Augustus was curiously cultured in other ways. During his reign, he established Dresden as one of the most beautiful of all the continental cities, amassing a collection of art and antiquity that was as substantial as his appetites!

Act Three: Prisoner

1 Walpole, Horace and Wright, John. *The Letters of Horace Walpole: Vol I, 1735-1748* (1842). Philadelphia: Lea and Blanchard, p. 76.

2 Henderson, Ernest F. *Side Lights on English History* (1900). New York: Henry Holt and Company, p. 241.

3 The Lady Suffolk Walpole refers to was Henrietta Howard, George II's long-term mistress.

4 Walpole, Horace (1840). *The Letters of Horace Walpole, Earl of Orford: Vol I*. London: Richard Bentley, p.61. There is no evidence to support Walpole's fanciful assertion.

5 Maurice, Count of Saxony, was born in 1696. He enjoyed a long and celebrated military career, eventually being appointed Marshal General of France. He died in 1750.

6 Coxe, William (1798). *Memoirs of the Life and Administration of Robert Walpole*. London: T Cadell, Jun, and W Davies, p.269.

7 Stepney to Cresset, *Dresden Despatch*, 24 July - 3 August 1694.

8 Stepney to Blathwayt, *Dresden Despatch*, 10 July - 20 July 1694.

9   Stepney to Blathwayt, *Dresden Despatch*, 21 August - 31 August 1694.

10 She was never without a noble jailer by any other name until her death. Charles Augustus von Bothmer took the role from 1702 to 1721 and Sigismund, Count Bergest, from 1721 until Sophia Dorothea's death.

11 Sophia Dorothea's household consisted of ladies and gentlemen-in-waiting and two pages, whilst amongst her domestic staff were two valets, fourteen footmen, twelve female servants, three cooks, a confectioner and baker and a butler, in addition to an armed garrison of forty soldiers.

12 *Post Man and the Historical Account* (London, England), July 30, 1700 – 1 August, 1700; Issue 784.

13 Figuelotte retired to bed with an agonising sore throat during a trip to Hanover and never recovered. Following her death, there were unsubstantiated rumours that she had been poisoned with diamond powder that caused her stomach to rupture.

14 George Augustus and his wife, Caroline of Ansbach, had four children by the time he left for England, with four more to come. Sophia Dorothea had given birth to five children by Frederick William at this point, though only two lived. The couple would later welcome nine further children, with eight of those reaching adulthood. Their fourth child would one day achieve fame as Frederick the Great.

15 When Sophia Dorothea learned that her daughter was due to pass by Ahlden, she ordered her household to prepare to receive her. Dressed in her finery, Sophia Dorothea waited... and waited. Her daughter's carriage drove straight past without so much as slowing.

16 Coxe, William (1816). *Memoirs of the Life and Administration of Robert Walpole*. London: Longman, Hurst, Rees, Orme & Brown, p. 262.

17 When a portrait that sounds remarkably similar to this one was exhibited in London as part of an exhibition commemorating the House of Guelph in 1890, *The Times* gave the following commentary:

'This picture [...] is said to represent the unfortunate Queen Sophia Dorothea. Every one has read the romantic and mysterious story of her unhappiness with her husband

and of her death in a fortress-prison, and it is therefore to be regretted that there is no absolutely undoubted portrait of her here. For this finely-painted full-length of a lady in Royal robes, with the Crown of England by her side, was certainly painted long after 1726, when Sophia Dorothea died. […] It is, of course, just possible that it may have been a posthumous portrait, commissioned by George II as a memorial of his mother; but evidence on this point, if it exists, has not yet been brought forward.'

The Times (London, England), Tuesday, 30 December, 1890; Issue 33208.

Appendix A: A Note on Letters
1   The Morning Post (London, England), Thursday, May 10, 1900; Issue 39916.

Index